AROUND THE WORLD SEARCH AND LEARN™
—— WORD SEARCH PUZZLE ——

JAMAICA

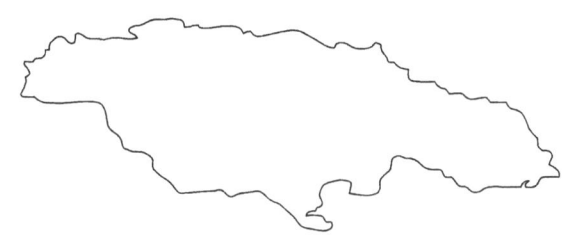

Elloree $\mathcal{P}$RESS

First published in the USA in 2025 by Elloree Press LLC
290 NW Peacock Blvd., #882125, Port St. Lucie, Florida 34988

Copyright © 2024 by Elloree Press LLC. All Rights Reserved. No part of this book may be reproduced or utilized in any form or by any means, electronic or mechanical, without express prior written permission in writing from the publisher.

ISBN: 978-0-9905193-4-8 (Paperback)

Cover and Design by: 120 Design Studio

Edited by: Kristi Irwin-Newberry

Printed and bound in the United States

Distribution in Jamaica via Dandelion House

The information in this book is for informational purposes only and you must use your own judgment and proceed at your own risk.

DISCLAIMER

Neither Elloree Press. nor any of their respective employees or agents will be held responsible for any accidents, losses, damages, wounds, sicknesses, delays, or irregularities that may occur during or because of the referrals or recommendations made in this book or by any defects, natural causes, or acts or negligence of people or companies which are referenced herein.

PREFACE

Welcome, fellow word search puzzle lovers!

I am thrilled to present you with a unique collection of puzzles that combine several of my passions—travel, culture, words, and learning.

This book is not just a compilation of puzzles; it's a labor of love and a reflection of my global experiences and personal journey around the world.

Since childhood, I have found joy and solace in word search puzzles. They are my way of relaxing, challenging myself, and keeping my mind sharp. I would often time myself, eager to beat my previous completion records. Over the years, this simple pastime has evolved into a cherished hobby that still brings me relaxation and satisfaction, especially when traveling. And now with the release of this series I have graduated to not just completing but creating puzzles as a way to relax.

It took me a few years to birth this idea. The inspiration for this travel word search series struck me while on vacation in Jamaica in 2018. One sunny afternoon, while lounging by the pool and soaking in the island's vibrant energy, I could not find an engaging word search book at the hotel gift shop. That's when the idea came to me—why not create a word search series that reflects my joy of travel and love of word search puzzles?

This book series is for all of you who find pleasure in words, exploration, and learning. It's designed to transport you to different destinations, each puzzle capturing the essence of a place.

Whether you're a seasoned traveler or someone who dreams of far-off lands, I hope this collection brings you as much joy and relaxation as it brought me while creating it.

Enjoy the adventure, one word at a time.

Valerie Irick Rainford

AROUND THE WORLD SEARCH AND LEARN™
—— WORD SEARCH PUZZLE ——

Around the World Search and Learn™ is your passport to discovering the world in whatever place uniquely gives you comfort. Each book in this collection takes you on a tour of a popular vacation destination, featuring word search puzzles that capture the essence of its culture, history, tourist attractions, cuisine, flora, and more.

Perfect for travelers, puzzle lovers, and anyone with a curiosity about the world, this collection offers hours of entertainment and education for all ages. Whether you're dreaming of sandy beaches or bustling city streets, these puzzles will transport you to far-off places while sharpening your mind. Your handy travel companion!

Celebrating Jamaica's Rich Tapestry Through Puzzles

It is my honor to introduce the world and my fellow Jamaicans to
'Around the World Search and Learn ™ - Jamaica.'

This exceptional puzzle book is a vibrant tribute to our island's rich history, captivating culture, and cherished traditions. Perfect for young minds and puzzle enthusiasts alike, it offers a delightful and educational experience that connects our people and captivates travelers from around the globe.

Each puzzle is a testament to the indomitable spirit of Jamaica, beautifully weaving together elements of our heritage, from iconic landmarks to culinary delights. I commend this initiative for enhancing cultural appreciation and supporting tourism, education, and community engagement.

Dive into these pages, and you'll find not just words, but the heartbeat of Jamaica.

Join me in celebrating our beautiful island in such an inspiring and entertaining manner."

Enjoy!

—R. OLIVER MAIR
Consulate General of Jamaica, Miami

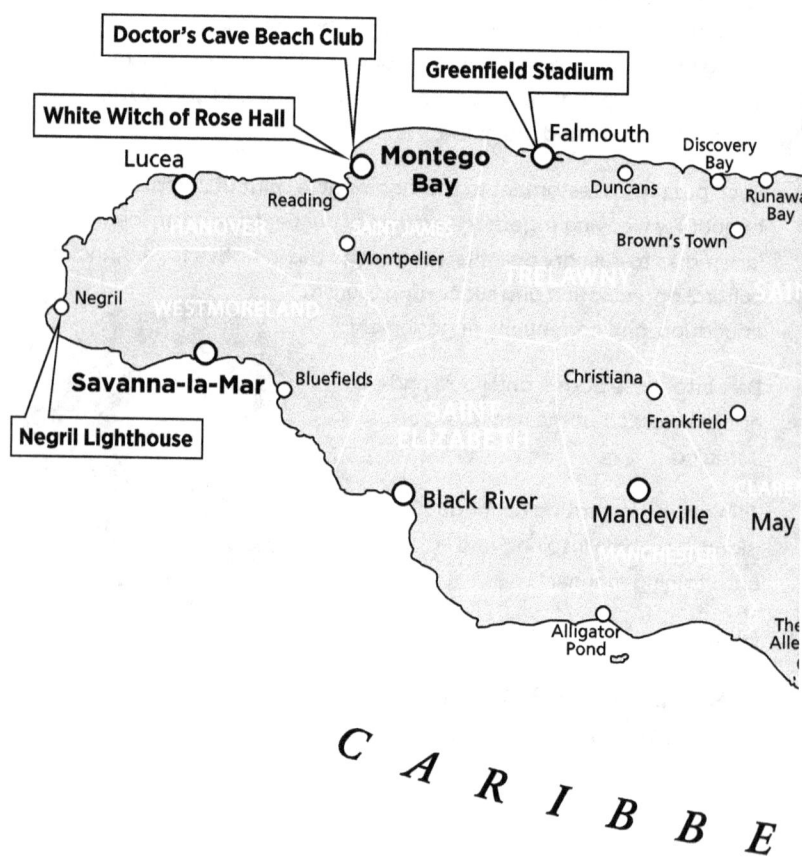

JAMAICA

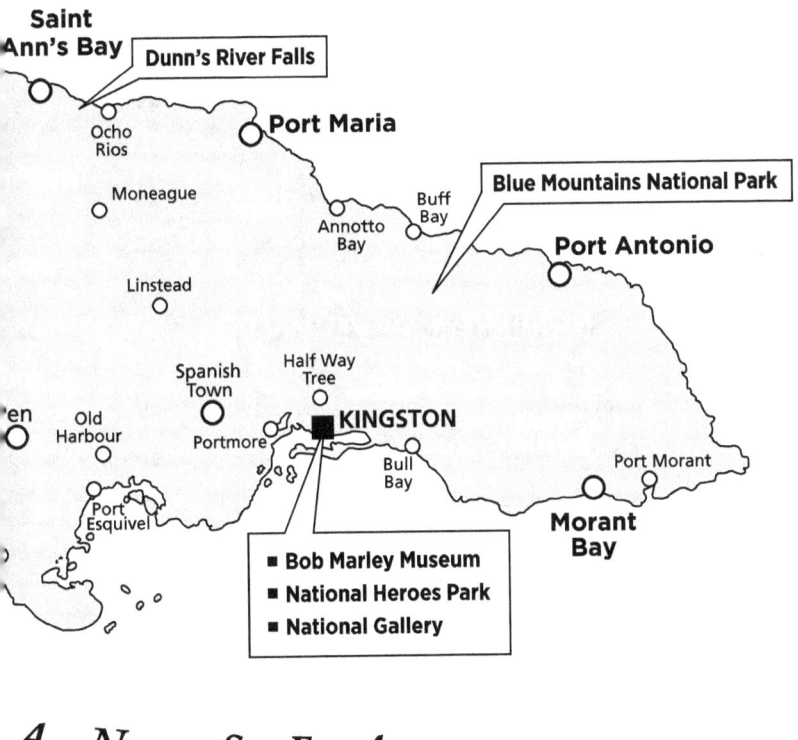

TABLE OF CONTENTS

SECTION 1: ABOUT JAMAICA

1. What to Expect................................10
2. History of Jamaica 12
3. Jamaica Is Known For......................14
4. Jamaican People............................16
5. Magic of Jamaica 18
6. Little Known Facts 20
7. Jamaica on Screen.........................22
8. Economy & International Trade.............24
9. Political Figures............................26

SECTION 2: FAMOUS JAMAICANS

10. Sam Sharpe................................28
11. Marcus Garvey.............................30
12. Bob Marley.................................32
13. Music Artists..............................34
14. Sports Icons...............................36
15. Usain Bolt.................................38
16. Roots in Jamaica..........................40

SECTION 3: JAMAICAN CULTURE

17. Food 42
18. Reggae Music 44
19. Rastafari 46
20. Art 48
21. Flowers 50
22. Organics 52
23. Patois 54

SECTION 4 : EXPLORING JAMAICA

24. Things to Do 56
25. Museums & Cultural Spaces 58
26. Festivals 60
27. Beaches 62
28. Water Activities 64
29. Kingston 66
30. Montego Bay 68
31. Rose Hall 70
32. Negril 72
33. Ocho Rios 74
34. Shopping 76
35. What to Pack 78
    Answers 81

1. WHAT TO EXPECT

Jamaica, with its **warm**, **vibrant culture** and **stunning** landscapes, offers a myriad of reasons to visit.

Start your **adventure** at the **breathtaking** Dunn's River Falls in **Ocho Rios**, where you can climb terraced cascades with **lush green** surroundings.

For a dose of **history** and colonial charm, visit Discovery **Bay** and the quirky **Giddy** House in **Port Royal**.

Nature enthusiasts will be captivated by the **Blue Mountains**, perfect for **hiking** and **coffee** tasting tours.

Don't miss the lively **music** and nightlife in **Kingston**, or the serene **beaches** of **Negril**, known for its crystal-clear waters and spectacular **sunsets**.

For a more laid-back vibe, explore the picturesque town of **Mandeville** or the **serene** beauty of Port **Antonio** and the **Rio Grande**.

With its blend of natural beauty, rich **heritage**, and warm **hospitality**, Jamaica promises an unforgettable experience.

WHAT TO EXPECT

```
B R E A T H T A K I N G Z S
L I N N K A H G N I K I H O
U O E T V F I C N H I M J I
E G E O P J S T E S N U S R
M R R N O A T N G Y G S E O
O A G I R M O A R D S I R H
U N N O T A R R I D T C E C
N D I M R I Y B L I O K N O
T E N R O C F I O G N L E E
A B N A Y A D V E N T U R E
I A U W A B E A C H E S V F
N Y T I L A T I P S O H O F
S W S M A N D E V I L L E O
H E R I T A G E R U T L U C
```

- Adventure
- Beaches
- Breathtaking
- Blue Mountains
- Coffee
- Culture
- Discovery **BAY**
- **GIDDY** House
- Green
- Heritage
- Hiking
- History
- Hospitality
- Jamaica
- Kingston
- Lush
- Mandeville
- Music
- Negril
- Ocho Rios
- Port **ANTONIO**
- Port Royal
- Rio Grande
- Serene
- Stunning
- Sunsets
- Vibrant
- Warm

2. HISTORY OF JAMAICA

The **colonization** of **Jamaica** began in 1655 when the **British** captured the island from the **Spanish**. This marked the start of a profound transformation characterized by the rise of plantation economies heavily reliant on the **transatlantic slave trade**.

Enslaved Africans were forcibly brought to Jamaica to work on **sugar**, **coffee**, and other cash crop plantations, creating significant economic wealth for British **colonists** at a tremendous human cost.

The cultural landscape of Jamaica was indelibly shaped by this period, as African traditions intermixed with **European** influences, giving rise to a rich tapestry of music, food, and folklore. The harsh realities of **slavery** eventually led to numerous uprisings and **revolts**, showcasing the **resilience** and **resistance** of the enslaved population.

British rule in Jamaica continued until 1962, culminating in the island's **independence** and the **liberty** of a **nation** rooted in a diverse cultural **heritage** and a complex **colonial history**.

HISTORY OF JAMAICA

```
R E S I L I E N C E R X N I
E E C O L O N I Z A T I O N
S G I O H S I T I R B I I D
I A T S L I B E R T Y Y T E
S T N L R O Z N J O R R A P
T I A A V R N G Y H E O N E
A R L I A A N I U J V T H N
N E T N J G A K S L A S E D
C H A O A U E N L T L I V E
E Q S L M S P A N I S H A N
Y P N O A B O V T S N D L C
T V A C I A R E V O L T S E
U O R M C R U B D O I R E P
S I T R A D E C E E F F O C
```

British
Coffee
Colonial
Colonists
Colonization
European
Heritage
History
Independence
Jamaica
Liberty
Nation
Resilience
Resistance
Revolts
Slave
Slavery
Spanish
Sugar
Trade
Transatlantic

3. JAMAICA IS KNOWN FOR

Renowned as the birthplace of **reggae** music and home to the legendary **Bob Marley**, Jamaica's soulful rhythms resonate through its bustling streets and serene **beaches**, capturing the essence of the culture. This vibrant **island** is not only a haven for **music** lovers but also a paradise for travel and cultural enthusiasts alike.

Visitors can unwind on its idyllic shores, from the world-famous Seven Mile Beach to the secluded **coves** of Treasure Beach, while enjoying the island's laid-back **vacation vibes**. Whether you're a **tourist** chasing the **sunset** or indulging in the island's rich **art** and culinary scene, there's something for everyone.

For those seeking a touch of adventure, exploring the Green Grotto **Caves** is a must-do experience that reveals Jamaica's natural **beauty**.

Coffee aficionados will delight in the robust flavors of **Blue Mountain** Coffee, grown in the island's **misty** highlands. Meanwhile, **food** lovers can savor **spicy jerk** dishes alongside a refreshing **Red Stripe beer**. And don't forget to try a freshly cracked **coconut** by the **ocean**, a perfect treat while basking in the sun.

Sports enthusiasts won't be disappointed either, with opportunities to experience exhilarating **track** and field or **cricket** events, play a round of golf, or catch a thrilling football match.

The friendly local **people** are always eager to share their love for these activities with visitors and tourists.

From savoring the finest **rum** or **mango** straight from the tree, to exploring Jamaica's **artistic** heritage, this scenic **Caribbean** Island promises an unforgettable experience filled with warmth, excitement, and vibrant cultural vibes. Whether you're seeking rest, relaxation, romance, or adventure, Jamaica has it all.

JAMAICA IS KNOWN FOR

```
R G O G C O G N A M I S T Y
R Y B L U E M O U N T A I N
E A I E T K M I C E Q K Y A
E C S E V O C T I K A C Y V
B R L T H S O A T U J A C P
E I A R A U F C S M N R I Y
P C N O R O F A I P A T P E
I K D I O B E V T D E B S L
R E S D K R E J R N B E L R
T T E S N U S E A M B A V A
S R P E O P L E R I I U E M
D A M U S I C N V M R T O B
E U T U N O C O C A A Y H O
R E G G A E A S E H C A E B
```

- Art
- Artistic
- Beaches
- Beauty
- Blue Mountain
- Bob Marley
- Caribbean
- Caves
- Coconut
- Coffee
- Coves
- Cricket
- Food
- Island
- Jerk
- Mango
- Misty
- Music
- Ocean
- People
- Red Stripe Beer
- Reggae
- Rum
- Spicy
- Sunset
- Tourist
- Track
- Vacation
- Vibes

4. JAMAICAN PEOPLE

The essence of Jamaica is a vibrant mix of **resilient** and **creative** people, deeply rooted in the rich cultural **heritage** of the **Caribbean**.

Jamaicans are known for their **easygoing**, **carefree** nature yet deeply **grateful** such that it permeates their daily lives, making them incredibly **appreciative** of the simple joys of life.

Jamaicans are incredibly **expressive**, with a zest for life that is both contagious and **inspiring**. Their **kind, warm, friendly** demeanor and **fun-loving** spirit make them naturally **generous** and **welcoming** to others.

Through the highs and lows, Jamaicans remain steadfast and **proud**, always finding ways to celebrate life with **passion** and **joy**.

Their unique combination of **calm** and **vibrant** personalities, coupled with an innate **respect** for others, creates an **irie** atmosphere that is truly captivating.

Don't worry, be **happy**!

In this casual yet lively environment, where the Caribbean sun meets the island's rhythmic beats, experiencing the culture feels like an adventure that enriches your soul and broadens your horizons.

JAMAICAN PEOPLE

```
A P P R E C I A T I V E A V
V A R A E A E V I T A E R C
A S O N N R E S I L I E N T
C S U O R E N E G U N N G D
J I D V L F D R N F S A N R
T O C Y H R E A I E P E I C
C N Y Y A E O V V T I B M A
E Y A H P E I A O A R B O L
P R R T P O R D L R I I C M
S E A S Y G O I N G N R L R
E G A T I R E H U I G A E A
R Y L D N E I R F R K C W W
O C T N A R B I V I F E I A
E V I S S E R P X E O N E R
```

Appreciative	Fun loving	Kind
Calm	Generous	Passion
Caribbean	Grateful	Proud
Carefree	Happy	Resilient
Creative	Heritage	Respect
Easygoing	Inspiring	Vibrant
Expressive	Irie	Warm
Friendly	Joy	Welcoming

5. MAGIC OF JAMAICA

Discover the magic of Jamaica, where breathtaking beaches meet lush greenery and vibrant culture. This island offers an extraordinary array of **attractions** that cater to every type of traveler, ensuring your visit is nothing short of spectacular.

Whether you're looking to **relax** on the **beach** under the warm **sun**, explore lively **art** scenes, or **indulge** in world-famous **cuisine**, Jamaica has something for everyone. Enjoy the pristine beaches, where you can **swim** in crystal-clear waters, **unwind** and perfect your **tan** by the pool, and then savor the local flavors that make this island a paradise for foodies.

After a day in the sun, you can **rest, recharge** and **rejuvenate** with a luxurious **spa massage** at a **resort** that caters to your every need, ensuring you drift off into the best **sleep** of your life.

For those seeking adventure, thrilling **excursions** await! **Tour** the majestic Blue Mountains, **explore** hidden waterfalls, and **experience** the thrill of river rafting. Each excursion promises **fun** and adventure, offering experiences that are as exhilarating as they are memorable.

Alongside these adventures, take time to celebrate the vibrant culture of Jamaica through its music, **dance**, and festivals. Dance to the rhythm of reggae, join a local **celebration** to connect with the warm, welcoming **people** who make Jamaica feel like a home away from home.

From exhilarating excursions to tranquil retreats, make your next **getaway** an adventure to remember. **Fall in love** with the enchanting **scenery** and vibrant **culture** that define this captivating destination. Whether you seek to unwind or seek adventure, Jamaica promises a **vacation** that leaves lasting memories and a yearning to return.

MAGIC OF JAMAICA

```
R E J U V E N A T E B S C I
E A H C A E B T O X A L E R
C E F D C J T T U C R E L S
H C T R A A S R R U T E E J
A N E E T P E A D R D P B E
R E G S I S R C N S P A R V
G I E O O T U T I I B S A O
E R H R N I T I W O E C T L
R E T T S N L O N N G E I N
O P A I N D U N U S A N O I
L X N O A U C S F M S E N L
P E Q N P L R K U I S R M L
X W C V X G E T A W A Y T A
E E L P O E P Y J S M L Z F
```

- Art
- Attractions
- Beach
- Celebration
- Cuisine
- Culture
- Dance
- Excursions
- Experience
- Explore
- Fall in Love
- Fun
- Get Away
- Indulge
- Massage
- People
- Recharge
- Rejuvenate
- Resort
- Relax
- Rest
- Scenery
- Sleep
- Spa
- Sun
- Swim
- Tan
- Tour
- Unwind
- Vacation

6. LITTLE KNOWN FACTS

Jamaica is a vibrant island nation known for its rhythmic reggae, pristine beaches, and rich history. While many are familiar with these features, here are a few facts you may not know:

- Jamaica's name is derived from the **Arawak** word "**Xaymaca**," meaning "Land of **Wood** and **Water**", reflecting the island's lush landscapes, abundant rivers, and breathtaking waterfalls.

- The **Maroons, descendants** of **enslaved** Africans who **escaped** from plantations, played a pivotal role in Jamaica's history. These resilient **ancestors** established autonomous societies in the island's mountains and were instrumental in resisting colonial rule.

- Jamaica's **motto**, "Out of Many, One People," reflects its diverse cultural heritage. The island's population is a blend of **African, European, Indian, Chinese,** and **Middle Eastern** ancestry.

- Jamaica is not only dotted with picturesque beaches but also abundant with natural **springs**. The island hosts more than 120 **rivers**, many originating from **underground** sources.

- Jamaica is the birthplace of the iconic **James Bond** series. Author Ian **Fleming** created the suave spy while staying at his Jamaican villa, **Goldeneye**, located in the small town of Oracabessa in Saint Mary Parish, east of Ocho Rios.

- Jamaica, home to more than 200 **species** of **birds**, is a **haven** for bird enthusiasts. This includes several endemic species, such as the Jamaican **Tody** and **Doctor Bird** (the national bird).

- Port Royal, once known as "the wickedest city on earth," was a bustling **hub** for **pirates** in the 17th century. It attracted notorious figures like Captain Henry Morgan.

LITTLE KNOWN FACTS

```
X E N S L A V E D A Q W D Y
S S S D O N A C I R F A N R
G C T R G A S R E V I R U Q
N A N I N E C H A V E N O S
I P A B I P I R A T E S R R
R E D R M O S D S H J Q G O
P D N O E R P A W A T E R T
S N E T L U E C R C I B E S
N A C C F E C H F A N U D E
O I S O L M I I X M W H N C
O D E D T W E N V Y O A U N
R N D N O B S E M A J T K A
A I A O D L O S N X P V T Z
M V D E Y E N E D L O G R O
```

- African
- Ancestors
- Arawak
- Birds
- Chinese
- Descendants
- Doctor Bird
- Enslaved
- Escaped
- European
- Fleming
- Goldeneye
- Haven
- Hub
- Indian
- James Bond
- Maroons
- Middle Eastern
- Motto
- Pirates
- Rivers
- Species
- Springs
- Tody
- Underground
- Water
- Wood
- Xaymaca

7. JAMAICA ON SCREEN

Jamaica, known for its lush landscapes and vibrant culture, has long been an alluring backdrop for **filmmakers** worldwide. The island's **cinematic** charm is evident in a range of **iconic films** made on the island.

One of the earliest examples is 20,000 Leagues Under the Sea (1954), which featured **scenes** along Jamaica's **picturesque** coastline. The James Bond series put Jamaica firmly on the cinematic map with **Dr. No** (1962), starring Sean Connery filmed in **breathtaking** places like Dunn's River Falls.

The **action**-packed spy film In Like **Flint** (1967) also showcased many of Jamaica's **exotic** locales. Meanwhile, The Harder They Come (1972), starring Jimmy Cliff, was filmed primarily in Kingston and remains a cultural **touchstone** that introduced reggae music to an **international** audience.

Clara's Heart (1988), featuring Whoopi Goldberg, captured the **scenic** beauty of Jamaica, while **Cool Runnings** (1993) brought the true story of the Jamaican bobsled team to life. Filmed partly in Discovery Bay and Montego Bay, the **movie** includes scenes of **stunning** beaches and **lively** markets in Jamaica.

The romantic **drama** How **Stella** Got Her Groove Back (1998), starring Angela Bassett and Taye Diggs, highlighted Jamaica's luxurious resorts and pristine beaches. **Pirates** of the **Caribbean**: The Curse of the Black Pearl (2003), featuring Johnny Depp as Captain Jack Sparrow, used Jamaica's breathtaking Port Royal as one of its key **locations**.

More recently, **Inna de Yard**: The Soul of Jamaica (2019) is a documentary that dives deep into the heart of Jamaican music, capturing its essence and influence.

JAMAICA ON SCREEN

```
C L A N O I T A N R E T N I
I A G N I K A T H T A E R B
N M R F I G N I N N U T S I
E D C I H T H D T F S T G N
C E S L B A M R N I E Y N N
S N E M I B D A I L N C I A
C O T M C A E M L M E I N D
I T A A O Y N A F S C T N E
T S R K N V L D N E S A U Y
O H I E I O I E O N H M R A
X C P R C L I E V O U E L R
E U Q S E R U T C I P N O D
I O S N O I T A C O L I O S
Q T R A E H S A R A L C C E
```

Action
Breathtaking
Caribbean
Cinematic
Claras Heart
Cool Runnings
Drama
Dr No
Exotic

Films
Filmmakers
Flint
Iconic
Inna de Yard
International
Lively
Locations
Movie

Picturesque
Pirates
Scenes
Scenic
Stella
Stunning
Touchstone

8. ECONOMY & INTERNATIONAL TRADE

With as many as 4.1 million tourists visiting annually, **tourism** is a primary **driver** in Jamaica's **economy**, generating a significant portion of its foreign exchange, and providing many jobs for the local population.

The financial sector, bolstered by a **robust** banking system and favorable investment climate, provides the backbone for both local entrepreneurs and international investors.

In addition, Jamaica has had strong **export** activities, prominently driven by **three key** products—**bauxite, coffee,** and **sugar**.

Jamaica's **vast** bauxite **reserves** cement its status in the **global mineral** export **sector**. Bauxite is a crucial **raw material** for aluminum **production**, placing Jamaica at the heart of an **industry** that supports economic growth and development.

Renowned worldwide for its **rich**, flavorful **Blue** Mountain Coffee, Jamaica caters to an **international** clientele that appreciates premium **quality**. This coffee is not just a product; it symbolizes Jamaican heritage and excellence.

Additionally, Jamaica's sugar industry has been a **vital** economic pillar, with farms producing high-quality **cane** sugar. The island's climate and landscapes are perfect for cultivating rich, sweet cane, making Jamaican sugar a sought-after product in the international **market**.

The **United States, Canada,** and **China** stand out as Jamaica's primary **trade** partners. These countries import significant quantities of Jamaican coffee, bauxite, and sugar, fostering robust international trade relationships.

ECONOMY & INTERNATIONAL TRADE

```
V C Y M O N O C E E F F O C
T A N L A R E N I M L E H A
S E C T O R R A Q I A I K N
A E O U I A K L R E N N E A
V Z D C T T S E E A O D Y D
M L H A S S Q R T S I U T A
A A J U R K H Z E T T S I M
T B B L A T I V R R A T L S
E O E A G Q R O E Q N R A I
R L K N U E P V R E R Y U R
I G V L S X I Z N A E O Q U
A R W E E R I A W T T U P O
L P R O D U C T I O N A L T
A S E T A T S D E T I N U B
```

Bauxite	Industry	Rich
Blue	International	Robust
Canada	Key	Sector
Cane	Market	Sugar
China	Material	Three
Coffee	Mineral	Tourism
Driver	Production	Trade
Economy	Quality	United States
Export	Raw	Vast
Global	Reserves	Vital

9. POLITICAL FIGURES

Jamaican politics is characterized by a robust **democratic** system with two major **political** parties—the Jamaica Labour Party (JLP) and the People's National **Party** (PNP). These parties have alternated **power** since Jamaica's independence in 1962.

The **JLP** was founded in 1943 by Sir Alexander **Bustamante**, the nation's first **Prime Minister**. The party's early focus on workers' rights and social welfare under Bustamante's leadership garnered significant **support** among Jamaica's working class. Hugh **Shearer**, another prominent JLP leader, served as Prime Minister from 1967 to 1972 and promoted an economic development **governance** agenda.

On the other side, the **PNP** was established in 1938 by **Norman** Manley, who also served as a pivotal figure in Jamaica's path to **independence**. His son, Michael **Manley** served during the 1970s pursuing nationalization of key industries and expansion of social services. P.J. **Patterson**, a long-serving leader of the PNP, was Prime Minister from 1992 to 2006 and was instrumental in modernizing Jamaica's infrastructure.

Over the years, notable leaders such as Edward **Seaga** served as Prime Minister from 1980 to 1989, implementing free market reforms. Donald **Sangster** briefly served as Prime Minister until his untimely death in 1967, leaving a legacy of industrializing the Jamaican **economy**. More recently, Portia **Simpson-Miller**, Jamaica's first female Prime Minister, left her mark by advocating for economic inclusivity and improved infrastructure.

Although less prominent, the National Democratic Movement (**NDM**), formed in 1995 by Bruce **Golding**, who later returned to JLP and became Prime Minister, also contributes to the island's political diversity. Andrew **Holness** the leader of the JLP and current Prime Minister is the youngest person to hold the office while the current **leader** of the opposition, the PNP, is Mark Golding.

POLITICAL FIGURES

```
H R E T S I N I M E M I R P
O V M S T R O P P U S A G O
L D A L N A C I A M A J N L
N E C N E D N E P E D N I I
E S C I T I L O P E R I D T
S P O W E R Y E L N A M L I
S H E A R E R R J O P E O C
A I R E D A E L S S E A G A
N O R M A N L E L R O R E L
G O V E R N A N C E R P E B
S N D E M O C R A T I C L C
T F E C O N O M Y T R A P L
E O R D E T N A M A T S U B
R E L L I M N O S P M I S E
```

Sir Alexander **BUSTAMANTE**
DEMOCRATIC
ECONOMY
Bruce **GOLDING**
GOVERNANCE
Andrew **HOLNESS**
INDEPENDENCE
JAMAICAN
Jamaica Labour Party (**JLP**)
LEADER
Michael **MANLEY**
National Democratic Movement (**NDM**)
NORMAN Manley
PARTY
P.J. **PATTERSON**
People's National Party (**PNP**)
POLITICAL
POLITICS
POWER
PRIME MINISTER
Donald **SANGSTER**
Edward **SEAGA**
Hugh **SHEARER**
Portia **SIMPSON-MILLER**
SUPPORT

10. SAM SHARPE

Sam Sharpe, also known as Samuel Sharpe, stands as a **revered** Jamaican national **hero** and **idol**.

Born into slavery in the early 19th century, Sharpe was a **Baptist deacon** who used his position to inspire and mobilize his fellow **enslaved** Africans towards **freedom**.

As a **leader**, he was **instrumental** in the organization of the widespread 1831 slave **rebellion**, also known as the Christmas Rebellion or Baptist **War**, which became a pivotal event in Jamaica's **history**.

Although the **uprising** was suppressed and Sharpe was **executed** in 1832, his **brave** efforts significantly hastened the abolition of slavery in **Jamaica**, which followed in 1834.

Today, Sam Sharpe is a **patriot** who is celebrated for his **unwavering** commitment to **justice** and human **dignity**, leaving an **indelible legacy** that continues to **inspire** generations of Jamaicans and history enthusiasts alike.

> *"I would rather die upon yonder gallows than live my life in slavery"*
>
> – **Sam Sharpe**

SAM SHARPE

```
R I U M S Y A C I A M A J S
E M R N E G N I S I R P U O
L A T N E M U R T S N I S R
I P G N I R E V A W N U T E
X M E A N L I Y R O T S I H
A O N N S P A T R I O T C N
Y D S E P R A H S M A S E O
T E L B I L E D N I D O L I
I E A A R L W N F A T Q E L
N R V Q E V M O B O B P F L
G F E A V U R C J Z R D A E
I S D R T D L A C N A W G B
D E T U C E X E K I V H A E
R Y C A G E L D E R E V E R
```

- Baptist
- Brave
- Deacon
- Dignity
- Enslaved
- Executed
- Freedom
- Hero
- History
- Idol
- Indelible
- Inspire
- Instrumental
- Jamaica
- Justice
- Leader
- Legacy
- Patriot
- Rebellion
- Revered
- Sam Sharpe
- Uprising
- Unwavering
- War

11. MARCUS GARVEY

Marcus Garvey, a towering figure in early 20th-century history, was a **Jamaican political leader, publisher, journalist,** and **orator** who championed the cause of **black nationalism** and Pan-Africanism.

Born on August 17, 1887, in **St. Ann's Bay**, Jamaica, Garvey founded the Universal Negro Improvement Association (**UNIA**) in 1914, which aimed to **uplift** people of African descent worldwide.

His powerful rhetoric and **visionary** ideas inspired millions, promoting **pride** in African heritage and advocating for economic **independence** and self-reliance.

Garvey's legacy endures through his profound influence on subsequent **civil rights** movements and his enduring call for **unity** among people of African descent.

Visitors to Jamaica can explore landmarks and museums dedicated to his memory, offering a deeper understanding of his **pivotal** role in shaping the **global struggle** for racial **equality** and **justice**.

> *"A people without the knowledge of their past history, origin and culture is like a tree without roots"*
>
> **- Marcus Garvey**

MARCUS GARVEY

```
Y R A N O I S I V A L A P R
E E C N E D N E P E D N I E
V S I M Y T I L A U Q E V D
R R V S T T P R I D E L O A
A Q I I I T U P L I F T T E
G N L L N S B H Q Y Y S A L
S E R A U I L G A R N S L A
U L I N E L I B O A R E A C
C G G O V A S C Z O C A B I
R G H I U N H P T I O L O T
A U T T N R E A T A A U L I
M R S A J U R S X C Y N G L
C T T N I O U R K F T I S O
E S O M C J A M A I C A N P
```

- Black
- Civil Rights
- Equality
- Global
- Independence
- Jamaican
- Journalist
- Justice
- Leader
- Marcus Garvey
- Nationalism
- Orator
- Pivotal
- Political
- Pride
- Publisher
- St. Ann's Bay
- Struggle
- UNIA
- Unity
- Uplift
- Visionary

12. BOB MARLEY

Bob Marley, born Robert **Nesta** Marley, is a **legendary** figure in the world of **music**, celebrated for his pioneering role in popularizing **reggae** globally. Born on February 6, 1945, in Nine Mile in Saint Ann parish, he later relocated to **Trenchtown**, Jamaica. Marley's music transcended cultural and geographical boundaries, delivering powerful messages of **love, peace**, and **resistance**.

His iconic tracks like "**Buffalo Soldier**," "Could You Be Loved," "**Get Up, Stand Up**," "I Shot the Sheriff," "**Is This Love**," "**Jamming**," "One Love," "**No Woman, No Cry**," "**Redemption Song**," and "Three Little Birds" have left an indelible mark on music history.

Beyond his solo achievements, Marley's collaborations with his band, The **Wailers**, and the influence of key figures like his wife **Rita Marley** and his son **Ziggy Marley**, further solidified his legacy.

Bob Marley's music not only entertained but also served as a **voice** for the marginalized, making him a **timeless** symbol of resistance and **unity**.

The Marley family legacy of music lives on in his children and grandchildren who have followed in his iconic footsteps in the world of music. For example, his sons Ziggy, Stephen, Julian, Ky-Mani and Damian Marley have made their mark in reggae and hip-hop, while his grandchildren YG, Jo Mersa, Bambatta, Daniel, Skip and Mystic Marley all have music careers as well.

> *"You never know how strong you are,*
> *until being strong is your only choice"*
>
> **- Bob Marley**

BOB MARLEY

```
G N O S N O I T P M E D E R
E O W A I L E R S L T Z C E
T W G O X A D W R E I W N I
U O R N T D O T E G M E A D
P M P S I H N Y G E E V T L
S A E Z R M C Y G N L O S O
T N A C Y C M N A D E L I S
A N C A I A M A E A S S S O
N O E I R O P G J R S I E L
D C S L S E V O L Y T H R A
U R E X T U S R L K C T X F
P Y E L R A M A T I R S O F
Y T B O E V O L E N O I Y U
O U N I T Y E L R A M B O B
```

- Bob Marley
- Buffalo Soldier
- Get Up Stand Up
- Is This Love
- Jamming
- Legendary
- Love
- Music
- Nesta
- No Woman No Cry
- One Love
- Peace
- Redemption Song
- Reggae
- Resistance
- Rita Marley
- Timeless
- Trenchtown
- Unity
- Voice
- Wailers
- Ziggy Marley

13. MUSIC ARTISTS

Jamaica has produced an array of iconic musicians whose influence spans the globe. **Bob Marley**, the legendary reggae musician, became a universal symbol of peace and resistance.

Shabba Ranks, known as the "Dancehall Emperor," brought a unique style and vocal delivery that helped elevate dancehall music on the international stage with hits like "Mr. Loverman".

Another pivotal figure in reggae and dancehall is **Buju Banton**, whose career spans decades and includes his hit "Boom Bye Bye" and later, socially conscious tracks like "Untold Stories".

Barrington Levy, Beenie Man, and **Yellowman** also brought Jamaican dancehall to international stages, while **Jimmy Cliff's** soulful tunes in "The Harder They Come" and "Many Rivers to Cross" introduced reggae to broader audiences.

Marcia Griffiths, known for her work with the I-Threes, Bob Marley's backup singers, gave us "Electric Boogie". **Gregory Isaacs**, the "Cool Ruler," serenaded fans with smooth, romantic reggae anthems.

Peter Tosh, another founding member of **The Wailers**, was known for his revolutionary lyrics, including songs like "Legalize It" and "Get Up, Stand Up". **Bunny Wailer's** influence in reggae includes classics like "Dreamland" and "Blackheart Man". **Shaggy** has achieved immense success both in reggae and pop genres with songs like "It Wasn't Me" and "Angel,"

Singer, Rapper and Songwriter, **Sean Paul** has played a crucial role in popularizing dancehall music worldwide with top tracks like "Get Busy" and "Temperature".

Ziggy Marley has carved out his own successful career with hits like "Love Is My Religion" and his work with the Melody Makers.

MUSIC ARTISTS

```
S H T I F F I R G A I C R A M
C M S U S B I S J C Y R E G G
A Y K E L E A H I R E A M E A
A J N A Z E C A M Z L S B H R
S E A R R N I G M U R R U S E
I N R O E I A G Y N A E J O L
Y A A F G E M Y C I M L U T I
R M B O B M A R L E Y I B R A
O W B N G A J S I T G A A E W
G O A I A N I U F Y G W N T Y
E L H A E R C U F M I E T E N
R L S E A N P A U L Z H O P N
G E D U S E G G R C I T N A U
M Y V E L N O T G N I R R A B
```

Barrington Levy
Beenie Man
Bob Marley
Buju Banton
Bunny Wailer
Gregory Isaacs
Jamaica
Jimmy Cliff
Marcia Griffiths
Peter Tosh
Sean Paul
Shabba Ranks
Shaggy
The Wailers
Yellowman
Ziggy Marley

14. SPORTS ICONS

Jamaica's rich tapestry of **sports** is woven with impressive achievements and legendary **athletes** who have left indelible marks on the **global** stage. In **track** and field, the island nation has produced sprinting **legends** like **Usain Bolt**, known as the fastest man alive, shattered world **records** and captivated audiences with his lightning **speed**. Shelly-Ann **Fraser-Pryce**, a dominant force in women's sprinting with multiple **Olympic** and World **Championship** titles. The legacy extends to Merlene **Ottey**, whose career spans five decades, making her one of the most decorated female **sprinters**.

Boxing has also seen its share of Jamaican champions, with Trevor **Berbick** who made history as a heavyweight boxing champion, famously defeating Muhammad Ali in 1981.

Cricket, another popular sport, boasts icons like Chris **Gayle**, known for his explosive batting, and Courtney **Walsh**, celebrated for his fast-bowling prowess. Adding to this illustrious **roster** is Jeff **Dujon**, whose skills behind the stumps and knack for strategic gameplay made him an integral part of the West Indies cricket **team** during their golden **era**.

Soccer, known as **Football** in Jamaica, also thrives, with the national team, the **Reggae Boyz**, qualifying for the **FIFA World Cup** in 1998, marking a significant milestone in the country's sporting history.

These athletes and achievements highlight Jamaica's profound impact on the world of sports, underscoring the nation's commitment to excellence and its ability to produce **world-class talent** across various disciplines.

SPORTS ICONS

```
L V E C Y R P R E S A R F D
E A A H R I E L A B O L G M
G R L A T H L E T E S R A L
E T E M L R Y E T T O E Y S
N R C P O T A L E N T B S S
D A I I B A G I N F O O P A
S C P O N O J U D S S X O L
D K M N I A G T E K C I R C
R C Y S A F N I W H A N T D
O I L H S I D E E P S G S L
C B O I U F O O T B A L L R
E R S P R I N T E R S E A O
R E T S O R P U C D L R O W
A B M Z Y O B E A G G E R Z
```

- Athletes
- Berbick
- Boxing
- Championship
- Cricket
- Dujon
- Era
- FIFA
- Football
- Fraser Pryce
- Gayle
- Global
- Legends
- Olympic
- Ottey
- Records
- Reggae Boyz
- Roster
- Speed
- Sports
- Sprinters
- Talent
- Team
- Track
- Usain Bolt
- Walsh
- World Class
- World Cup

15. USAIN BOLT

Usain St. Leo Bolt's name is synonymous with **speed, success**, and the spirit of Jamaica.

Born in the rural parish of **Trelawny**, Jamaica, Bolt's **rise** to international fame has cemented his status as the **greatest** sprinter of all time and made him a **hero** to Jamaican people.

Standing at 6'5" tall, Bolt's commanding presence is as **formidable** as his nickname, **"Lightning Bolt,"** suggests. Over the course of his career, he has consistently defied the limits of human speed, **set** world records and earned eight Olympic **gold** medals.

Bolt's unparalleled achievements include winning gold medals at three consecutive Olympic Games—**Beijing** 2008, **London** 2012, and **Rio de Janeiro** 2016—over a span of eight years.

At the Rio 2016 Games, he was the first athlete to win the 100-meter, 200-meter, and 4 × 100-meter relay events at three successive **Olympics**.

Beyond his athletic prowess, Bolt's **charisma** and **sportsmanship** have endeared him to fans around the globe. For Jamaicans, Bolt embodies national **pride** and **resilience**, often crediting his homeland for the **grit** and **determination** that fueled his success.

In addition to his athletic success, Bolt's **influence** extends beyond the **track**. Through his philanthropic endeavors, he gives back to the **community** that shaped him and uses his platform to support **youth** programs in Jamaica.

Usain Bolt's legacy is not just measured in **medals** and **records** but in the **hope**, he instills in young athletes **worldwide**.

"Don't think about the start of the race, think about the ending"

- **Usain Bolt**

USAIN BOLT

```
T I R G R E A T E S T W I W
R I S E T F B L O N D O N N
A T S R Q O J O H O L R F O
C L E E A R Z B T R O L L I
K O C S M M C G U I G D U T
H B C I S I O N O E D W E A
G R U L I D M I Y N S I N N
N E S I R A M N N A C D C I
I C L E A B U T W J I E E M
J O A N H L N H A E P O D R
I R D C C E I G L D M R I E
E D E E P S T I E O Y E R T
B S M O V E Y L R I L H P E
P I H S N A M S T R O P S D
```

Beijing
Charisma
Community
Determination
Formidable
Gold
Greatest
Grit
Hero
Hope

Influence
Lightning Bolt
London
Medals
Olympics
Pride
Records
Resilience
Rio de Janeiro

Rise
Set
Speed
Sportsmanship
Success
Track
Trelawny
Worldwide
Youth

16. ROOTS IN JAMAICA

At the heart of Jamaica's **global** cultural **impact** lies the Jamaican **diaspora**, whose reach extends far beyond the island's shores.

Among this expansive community are individuals we might refer to as "**Almost Jamaicans**"—those who are not Jamaican by nationality but share a **proud** connection through their **family** roots.

U.S. Vice President **Kamala** Harris exemplifies this legacy. Her father, Donald Harris, is Jamaican, and Kamala often credits her **heritage** for shaping her **values**.

Harry Belafonte, the iconic singer and activist, celebrated his Jamaican roots in his music, notably with "Banana Boat Song (Day-O)." His Jamaican **roots** informed his artistic expression and advocacy for civil rights.

The entertainment industry is replete with "Almost Jamaicans", and actress **Sheryl Lee Ralph**, daughter of Jamaican designer Ivy Ralph, proudly highlights her heritage in her career.

In sports, Basketball Hall of Famer **Patrick Ewing** attributes his success to the Jamaican **work ethic** instilled by his **parents**.

Colin Powell, the first African American Secretary of State, brought **honor** to both America and Jamaica. He frequently acknowledged his Jamaican immigrant parents' **influence** on his **leadership**.

Musicians like **Heavy D**, **Busta Rhymes**, and **The Notorious B.I.G.** embraced their Jamaican heritage, integrating its rhythms into their pioneering hip-hop music.

ROOTS IN JAMAICA

```
G L O B U S T A R H Y M E S
I L E A D E R S H I P H T G
B E O R G I M P A C T O N N
S W I B I G A R Q P O H O I
U O N K A V F S V R R A F W
O P F M A L A A P E Z L A E
I N L S R I M L T O O A L K
R I U N O E I O U T R M E C
O L E A N G L O S E H A B I
T O N C O A Y Q M T S K Y R
O C C I H T E K R O W H R T
N B E A A I D U O R P Y R A
E S P M U R X S T N E R A P
H P L A R E E L L Y R E H S
T B P J H H E A V Y D M A K
```

Almost
Busta Rhymes
Colin Powell
Diaspora
Family
Global
Harry Belafonte
Heavy D
Heritage
Honor
Impact
Influence
Jamaicans
Kamala
Leadership
Parents
Patrick Ewing
Proud
Roots
Sheryl Lee Ralph
The Notorious B.I.G.
Values
Work Ethic

17. FOOD

Jamaican cuisine is a vibrant, flavorful tapestry that reflects the island's rich cultural history and diverse culinary influences.

Start your day with a traditional Jamaican breakfast of **porridge** or **ackee** and **saltfish**, the national dish, which can also be eaten any time of day.

Later in the day, for those who love chicken, try Jamaican fry chicken with perfectly spiced crunch, while fricassee – or "**brown stew**" - chicken presents a tender, sauce-infused alternative. **Oxtail** or **stew peas** and rice will make your mouth water.

Curry goat, slow-cooked with a medley of spices, is a local favorite, while **escovitch fish** marinated in tangy vinegar sauce is a seafood lover's delight. For a milder option, mackerel served with **hard dough** bread is hearty and satisfying. Jamaican soups like **cow cod** or **cock soup**, along with goat-based **Manish water** or **Fish Tea**, are renowned for their bold, comforting flavors.

Traditional sides such as **bammy**, **breadfruit**, green **banana**, and **yam** complement these dishes beautifully, while dumplings and **cow foot** stew provide added texture and substance. **Rice and Peas** combines with absolutely everything. Don't forget to try a delicious spicy beef **patty** paired perfectly with soft and tasty coco bread.

No exploration of Jamaican cuisine is complete without **jerk**, a seasoning method that combines allspice and **Scotch bonnet** peppers for aromatic heat. Coconut milk infuses dishes with distinctive flavors, and sweet **mango** or refreshing **sorrel** drink balances the cuisine's richness. Have a piece of **bulla** cake with a cup of tea. Round out the day with a slice of **rum cake**, infused with Jamaican rum, for dessert.

FOOD

```
Y T E N N O B H C T O C S K
H I E W G X S T E W P E A S
S U K R E J R K E N E R E W
I R A C S A L T F I S H P R
F F C O C K S O U P S I D E
H D M W A N C L L T N G N T
C A U C W F I S H T E A A A
T E R O B A N A N A S I E W
I R R D T A O G Y R R U C H
V B O X D P A T T Y Q B I S
O C O W F O O T B A M N R I
C W P A L L U B A M M Y L N
S O R R E L B G B E E K C A
E G D I R R O P H O G N A M
```

- Ackee
- Bammy
- Banana
- Breadfruit
- Brown Stew
- Bulla
- Cock Soup
- Cow Cod
- Cow Foot
- Curry Goat
- Escovitch Fish
- Fish Tea
- Hard Dough
- Jerk
- Mango
- Manish Water
- Oxtail
- Patty
- Porridge
- Rice and Peas
- Rum Cake
- Salt Fish
- Scotch Bonnet
- Sorrel
- Stew Peas
- Yam

18. REGGAE MUSIC

Reggae music, the heartbeat of Jamaica, has given the world a treasure **trove** of unforgettable **hits**, each resonating with the island's rich cultural **rhythms** and heartfelt messages. Iconic **songs** like Bob Marley's **"One Love,"** **"No Woman, No Cry,"** and "Redemption Song" have become **anthems** of **peace** and resilience, reflecting the struggles and triumphs of the Jamaican people.

Reggae's profound influence also shines through in **tracks** like **"Israelites"** by Desmond Dekker, **"Legalize It"** by Peter Tosh, and Jimmy Cliff's soulful "Many Rivers to Cross." UB40's **"Red Red Wine"** and **"Kingston Town"** celebrate reggae's **global** appeal, while hits like **"Oh Carolina"** by Shaggy and **"Pass the Dutchie"** by Musical Youth bring infectious rhythms to the **dance** floor.

"Now That We've Found Love" by **Third World** and "Wild World" by **Maxi** Priest showcase the genre's versatility, blending **soulful** melodies with reggae's signature **beats**.

The genre's enduring legacy continues to inspire and **uplift**, uniting fans across the globe with its timeless message of **love**, **unity**, and social **justice**.

REGGAE MUSIC

```
H S G N O S K C A R T Z M O
A I S R A E L I T E S C F Y
T X T E N C T S M H T Y H R
H A A D T I F U P L O V E C
I M E R H T I M E E U G O O
R T B E E S L S A G G N H N
D G Y D M U P T C A E P C N
W L T W S J U I E L L E A A
O O I I R C V H O I U C R M
R B N N T R O V E Z F N O O
L A U E I X E G T E L A L W
D L R O W D L I W I U D I O
W K I N G S T O N T O W N N
E I H C T U D E H T S S A P
```

Anthems
Beats
Dance
Global
Hits
Israelites
Justice
Kingston Town
Legalize It
Love
Maxi
Music
No Woman, No Cry
Oh Carolina
One Love
Pass the Dutchie
Peace
Red Red Wine
Reggae
Rhythms
Songs
Soulful
Third World
Tracks
Trove
Unity
Uplift
Wild World

19. RASTAFARI

The **Rastafarian** community in **Jamaica** is a vibrant **cultural** and **spiritual movement** rooted in the principles of **Black pride** and **liberation**.

Emerging in the early 20th century, Rastafarianism was influenced by the teachings of **Marcus Garvey** whose advocacy for Pan-Africanism and Black self-empowerment became a foundational pillar for the movement.

Garvey's prophecy of a great African king being crowned was fulfilled in the eyes of Rastafarians with the coronation of **Haile Selassie** I of Ethiopia in 1930. Revered as the **living** embodiment of **Jah** (God), Selassie's legacy and titles, such as "**Lion of Judah**," became central to Rastafarian beliefs.

Rastafarianism provided a spiritual and cultural framework for a community that yearned to reclaim its **African** heritage and identity. Practices such as the wearing of dreadlocks reflect a connection to Rastafarian belief in living naturally and biblically. **Dreadlocks** are also a **symbol** of strength and **resilience**, reflecting the Revered Lion of Judah. The **Star of David**, along with titles like **Kingsmen** and **Queen**, reflects the **deep**-rooted honor and respect within the community.

Iconic figures like **Bob Marley** brought global recognition to Rastafarianism, spreading its messages of **peace** and **unity** through **reggae** music.

For cultural enthusiasts, members of the Jamaican diaspora, and history buffs, and the **Rasta** movement offers insight into the resilience, spirituality, and cultural richness of Jamaica.

RASTAFARI

```
A F R I C A N E M S G N I K
U T N E M E V O M K E H A J
Y N O R J A M A I C A S Y I
E K I L O B M Y S O G P E L
V R T T G N I V I L G I L I
R E A S Y T I R I D E R R O
A S R R A S T A F A R I A N
G I E R P E Q B W E A T M O
S L B Y E U J P I R S U B F
U I I P E A C E N D T A O J
C E L E D I R P K C A L B U
R N N S T A R O F D A V I D
A C U L T U R A L M C W E A
M E I S S A L E S E L I A H
```

- African
- Black Pride
- Bob Marley
- Cultural
- Deep
- Dreadlocks
- Haile Selassie
- Jah
- Jamaica
- Kingsmen
- Liberation
- Lion of Judah
- Living
- Marcus Garvey
- Movement
- Queen
- Peace
- Rasta
- Rastafarian
- Reggae
- Resilience
- Spiritual
- Star of David
- Symbol
- Unity

20. JAMAICAN ART

Jamaica's **vibrant art** scene provides a **unique** touch to the island's **cultural tapestry**.

Carl Abrahams, a pioneer in Jamaican art, is celebrated for his evocative and **colorful** religious and historical scenes. Cecil Baugh, primarily known for his **ceramics**, also made a significant impact with his **paintings**, reflecting the beauty of Jamaican landscapes.

David Boxer, both an **artist** and a **curator**, played a crucial role in establishing the National **Gallery** of Jamaica and promoting Jamaican art internationally. Hope Brooks' **abstract** works capture the essence of Jamaican **life** and environment, while Ralph Campbell is known for his **expressive** depictions of rural **scenes** and folklore.

Alexander Cooper's vibrant portraits and **genre** scenes bring to life the diverse **experiences** of Jamaicans. John Dunkley's haunting and surreal **landscapes** offer a deep, introspective view of the island's psyche. Milton George's bold use of **color** and form pushes the boundaries of traditional Jamaican art. Albert Huie, regarded as the father of Jamaican painting, brought international recognition to Jamaican art with **vivid** depictions of everyday life.

Eugene Hyde's **modernist** approach and innovative techniques have influenced a generation of Jamaican artists. Edna Manley, known as the mother of Jamaican art, provided powerful **sculptures** that reflect the strength and resilience of the Jamaican spirit. Alvin Marriott, a highly regarded sculptor, captured the **vibrancy** of Jamaican culture through his intricate works. Gaston Tabois is celebrated for a **style** that vividly portrays scenes of Jamaican life, embedding **humor** and **warmth** in his works.

Barrington Watson's masterful technique brought a sophisticated **edge** with his portrayal of human figures and historical scenes. Osmond Watson's bold colors and **striking** compositions convey a deep spirituality and cultural pride. Together, these artists have not only defined but also continually redefined Jamaican art, making an indelible mark on both local and global cultural landscapes.

JAMAICAN ART

```
Y R E L L A G N I K I R T S
R O M U H M O D E R N I S T
Q L V C E R A M I C S O R H
C O L O R F U L R V R A Y L
S C U L P T U R E S I E T A
G U N I Y C N A R B I V C R
N R I F S C E N E S I I A U
I A Q E A R W L A B O S R T
T T U L N A Y I R D E S T L
N O E E R T E A F O G E S U
I R G M S I N N R D D R B C
A R T I S T Y R T S E P A T
P H S E C N E I R E P X E A
E R Z L A N D S C A P E S N
```

- Abstract
- Art
- Artist
- Ceramics
- Color
- Colorful
- Cultural
- Curator
- Edge
- Experiences
- Expressive
- Gallery
- Genre
- Humor
- Landscapes
- Life
- Modernist
- Paintings
- Scenes
- Sculptures
- Striking
- Style
- Tapestry
- Unique
- Vibrancy
- Vibrant
- Vivid
- Warmth

21. FLOWERS

Jamaica is a treasure trove of vibrant tropical flora.

Amidst the island's lush landscapes, you can find stunning blooms such as the **Hibiscus**, known for its large petals that range from deep reds to bright yellows. Or the beautiful **Poinsettia**, known to many as the Christmas plant, enjoyed year-round in Jamaica.

The exotic **Bird of Paradise** dazzles with its striking resemblance to a bird in flight. Another highlight is the **Poinciana**, often referred to as the Flame Tree, which bursts into a fiery display of red and orange flowers.

Jamaica is home to an array of unique flowers including the **Lignum Vitae**, Blue **Mahoe**, **Bougainvillea**, **Heliconia**, **Orchid**, Ginger Lily, **Ixora**, **Frangipani**, **Croton**, and **Allamanda**. Majestic **Elephant Ear** plants, with their large, heart-shaped leaves, create a striking backdrop in many gardens.

Adding further diversity is the Trumpet Bush, known for its unique-shaped yellow flowers, and Wild **Jasmine**, fills the air with its sweet fragrance. The Yellow **Torch Ginger** stands tall with its bright blooms, while the Spider Lily has an intricate, web-like flower.

The **Jacaranda** tree, with its vibrant violet flowers, adds a splash of color to the countryside, signaling the arrival of cooler days.

The playful Parrot's Beak mimics the bright flowers of the jacaranda tree, while the **Plumeria**, famed for its intoxicating fragrance and beautiful white or pink flowers, is used to make traditional leis.

The **Purple Heart** provides a deep, velvety contrast in many gardens, while Purple **Sage** adds a soft, aromatic hue.

Meanwhile, the Silver **Palm** and Cactus thrive in the arid, sun-drenched regions of the island. The **Fern** and **Wild Pine** can be found creating dense, green carpets across the forest floor.

FLOWERS

```
H A I R E M U L P P N R E F
E L T A H O I R U O H T N A
R L O E P J I H R I E O I E
L A F T M A N I P N L R P L
I M J N V S A B L S E C D L
G A A A M P I E E C H L I
N N C H E I I S H T O G I V
U D A P O N G C E T N I W N
M A R E K E N U A I I N L I
V E A L A T A S R A A G A A
I N N E E C R O T O N E R G
T O D G B E F D I H C R O U
A N A I C N I O P A L M X O
E S I D A R A P F O D R I B
```

- Allamanda
- Bird of Paradise
- Bougainvillea
- Croton
- Elephant Ear
- Fern
- Frangipani
- Heleconia
- Hibiscus
- Ixora
- Jacaranda
- Jasmine
- Lignum Vitae
- Mahoe
- Orchid
- Palm
- Plumeria
- Poinciana
- Poinsettia
- Purple Heart
- Sage
- Torch Ginger
- Wild Pine

22. ORGANICS

Jamaica is a treasure trove of edible flora **organic** to the island.

Among the most celebrated are **ackee**, the national fruit, which is often paired with saltfish in the island's signature dish.

Breadfruit, introduced by Captain Bligh, serves as a versatile staple, roasted or fried to perfection. **Callaloo**, similar to spinach, is a leafy green packed with nutrients and commonly used in soups and stews. The island's bounty doesn't stop there; **avocado** (pear) provides healthy fats, while **guava** and **June plum** are rich in vitamins and antioxidants.

Mango offers a sweet, juicy treat that's hard to resist, and **naseberry** (sapodilla) brings a unique, caramel-like flavor. **Papaya** aids digestion and boosts immunity, while the exotic **star apple** adds a creamy texture to desserts. **Sorrel**, particularly popular during the Christmas season, is used to make a refreshing, tangy drink. **Soursop** is known for its potential health benefits, including immune support and anti-inflammatory properties.

Finally, Jamaican **coffee**, particularly from the Blue Mountains, is renowned worldwide for its exceptional quality and flavor.

Jamaican Pimento (**Allspice**) is a vital component of Jamaica's culinary identity. With an aroma that combines the sweet spices of cinnamon, cloves, and nutmeg, pimento is used extensively in jerk seasoning.

Coconut plays a versatile role in Jamaican cuisine, from use in cooking oil and milk to a base for curries and rice dishes. **Jackfruit** is a massive fruit with a flavor somewhere between bananas and pineapple. **Tamarind** is a sweet and sour pulpy fruit utilized in both savory and sweet dishes and also candies. **Bammy**, made from cassava, is a traditional flatbread often enjoyed fried alongside fish.

ORGANICS

```
M T I U R F D A E R B
E L P P A R A T S A A
V E S A Y A P A P V M
Q O E C I S L L A M
R O S O U R S O P U Y
Y L I N G V N E M G T
R A E N A N O Y R T I
R L Z M I D A N A U U
E L G N A I R M I N R
B A T C I N A G R O F
E C O L E R R O S C K
S V A H I E E F F O C
A T E N E R E E K C A
N M D M U L P E N U J
```

Ackee
Allspice
Avocado
Bammy
Breadfruit
Callaloo
Coconut
Coffee
Guava
Jackfruit
June Plum
Mango
Naseberry
Organic
Papaya
Sorrel
Soursop
Star Apple
Tamarind

23. PATOIS

Jamaican Patois is an English-based creole language with influences from West African and other languages, spoken primarily in Jamaica and among the Jamaican diaspora – Source: Wikipedia

Wah gwaan, mi **bredrin**! Mi waan fi chat u up bout mi homeland here inna Jamaica. Dis island weh full a vibes ya see. Mi people dem weh mek yuh feel right at home. **A beg yuh**, tek a sit and listen for a **likkle** bit.

First off, di beauty a Jamaica cyan be undaestimated. From di blue **wata** a di Caribbean Sea to di lush hills a di Blue Mountains, **evryweh** yuh look, it's a paradise. **Gwan** climb di Dunn's River or relax **pon** di Negril beach—**Evryting Irie**. Di sun shining bright, di breeze a blow cool, an nature just a work it magic pon di land.

Di culture a Jamaica is like no adda—rich an vibrant wid nuff history. Wi people chat inna wi sweet **Patwa**, an wi music? **Jessum** Peace, it **mash up** di world! From di roots a reggae music wid legends like Bob Marley to di dancehall riddims wha mek yuh waan move, music a part a wi soul.

Ya Mon, di people a Jamaica a di heart and soul a di island. No matta weh yuh come from, yuh get nuff respect and one love from di people dem. Wi lively, full a spirit, an always ready fi **give tanks** fi di blessings we have. Di Jamaican people carry dem culture wid pride, an dem **pickney** dem a grow up strong and proud a dem roots. Don't worry if **tings** nuh perfect—**no problem mon**, wi always find a way fi mek tings work.

Di essence a Jamaica cyan be explain inna no book or movie, yuh haffi feel it fi know it. **Soon come** visit, nuh **lef me nuh**, an mek sure fi **big up** the culture and di people dem wherever yuh deh. **One love, walk good**, and memba seh di best always soon come.

PATOIS

```
R A B D I E M O C N O O S
N O P R O B L E M M O N K
I O I A E O T I N G S E N
N E C N T D G F K R V L A
J V K E A W R K D K A O T
N R N E L L A I L A L V E
A Y E R M E Y T N A M E V
A T Y A U I F S O C W V I
W I A V S W P M S N A R G
G N M A S H U P E A Y Y W
H G O S E I G I E N A W A
A E N T J N I S U S U E N
W A T A D A B E G Y U H Z
```

- A Beg Yuh
- Big Up
- Bredrin
- Evryting
- Evryweh
- Give Tanks
- Gwan
- Irie
- Jessum
- Lef Me Nuh
- Likkle
- Mash Up
- No Problem Mon
- One Love
- Patwa
- Pon
- Pickney
- Soon Come
- Tings
- Wah Gwaan
- Walk Good
- Wata
- Ya Mon

24. THINGS TO DO IN JAMAICA

Jamaica offers a vibrant mix of activities that cater to all types of travelers.

Enhance your adrenaline-filled day with a **fishing** trip along the coastline, where the clear Caribbean waters teeming with fish provide an incredible catch and tale to tell.

For those seeking adventure, **zip-line** through the lush canopies at **Mystic Mountain** or **rafting** down the Martha Brae River are must-do experiences.

Nature lovers can go **hiking** through the verdant Blue Mountains or explore the serene **Rainforest**. **Scuba** diving and **snorkeling** in Jamaica's crystal-clear waters reveal a mesmerizing underwater world.

Culture enthusiasts will enjoy the rich history **tours** and the bustling **Craft Market** where they can find unique souvenirs.

Don't miss out on the **Appleton Estate** tour for a taste of authentic Jamaican **rum** or an exhilarating **bobsled** ride.

For a more relaxed experience, **sunbathe** on the pristine beaches, making sure to get that perfect **tan**, take a refreshing dip in the turquoise waters, or **sail** on a **catamaran**. With the sun gently warming your skin, it's the perfect place to relax and rejuvenate.

The night comes alive with street **parties**, **night clubs**, and the vibrant **art walk**.

Whether you're watching a **cricket** match or **swimming** with dolphins at **Dolphin Cove**, Jamaica promises an unforgettable adventure.

THINGS TO DO IN JAMAICA

```
E R E D J A M A I C A E M B
V P G B H W Y P R A B O S K
O O N H I L S P D T U C B A
C R I C K E T L E A C T U C
N A L X I H I E L M S S L R
I F E Z N T C T S A G E C A
H T K C G A M O B R N R T F
P I R S N B O N O A I O H T
L N O E I N U E B N M F G M
O G N I H U N S M L M N I A
D W S T S S T U T I I N R
O N C R I I A A R T W A L K
Y A K A F Q I T N O S R S E
M Z I P L I N E J S R U O T
```

Appleton Estate	Hiking	Sail
Art Walk	Jamaica	Scuba
Bobsled	Mystic Mountain	Snorkeling
Catamaran	Night Clubs	Swimming
Craft Market	Parties	Sunbathe
Cricket	Rafting	Tan
Dolphin Cove	Rainforest	Tours
Fishing	Rum	Zip Line

25. MUSEUMS AND CULTURAL SPACES

Jamaica is home to a vibrant tapestry of museums and places that offer a deep dive into its rich cultural heritage, making it a must-visit for any tourist.

Emancipation Park in the heart of Kingston honors the island's freedom from slavery. The **Bob Marley** Museum celebrates the reggae legend's life and **music**, housed in his former residence and studio. The **National Gallery** of Jamaica is a **cultural centre** showcasing works from Jamaica's most celebrated artists.

Liberty Hall pays tribute to Marcus Garvey, a key figure in Jamaican **history**, and offers an engaging multimedia experience about his life and philosophies.

The Institute of Jamaica stands as the country's cultural repository, featuring diverse exhibits on natural history, **ethnography**, and **art**.

For a taste of colonial architecture and history, the **Greenwood** Great House offers a glimpse into **plantation** life with its well-preserved **artifacts, scenic** views and beautiful **gardens**. Another notable historical landmark is the **Rose Hall** Great House.

Music enthusiasts will also appreciate the **Peter Tosh** Museum, dedicated to the life and legacy of the influential reggae musician and activist. History buffs can explore **Rio Nuevo**, the site of the last battle between the British and Spanish forces in Jamaica.

Finally, **Trench Town** Culture Yard provides an authentic look into the community where reggae was born, showcasing Bob Marley's early life and the **roots** of this globally influential music genre.

For those visiting **Devon** House, one of the island's most iconic landmarks, you'll find it not only rich in history but also a central spot to experience Jamaican culture.

MUSEUMS AND CULTURAL SPACES

```
U G Y H P A R G O N H T E
D A R T O L O N O V E D R
O L V H V X O W L E L E T
O L Q S E M T O L L A G N
W E Y O U N S T A P N S E
N R E T N O L H H C O T C
E Y L R O I Y C E I I C L
E R R E I T I N S N T A A
R O A T R A E E O E A F R
G T M E L T F R R C N I U
P S B P R N E T S S C T T
O I O M G A R D E N S R L
L H B Y D L M U S I C A U
N O I T A P I C N A M E C
```

- Art
- Artifacts
- Bob Marley
- Cultural Centre
- Devon
- Emancipation
- Ethnography
- Gallery
- Gardens
- Greenwood
- History
- Liberty Hall
- Music
- National
- Peter Tosh
- Plantation
- Rio Nuevo
- Roots
- Rose Hall
- Scenic
- Trench Town

26. FESTIVALS

Make sure to time your visit to Jamaica during a favorite festival.

There are many to choose from year-round. Kickstart your Jamaican adventure with the high-energy celebration of **Carnival**. Usually held in April, Carnival in Jamaica is a **dazzling** explosion of **music, dance,** and vibrant **costumes**.

Known as the largest concert festival in Jamaica, Reggae **Sumfest** is a must-visit for music lovers. Taking place in Montego Bay in July, this **festival** celebrates the world-renowned top **reggae** and **dancehall** artists.

For those seeking an unforgettable summer party **experience**, Dream Weekend in Negril is the place to be in August, featuring a series of themed parties and great **tunes** on the beach.

Look for music events and **performances** that emphasize different genres including **jazz**, reggae, SKA and dancehall. In February, the streets of Kingston come alive during Reggae Month in **tribute** and **celebration** of Jamaica's most iconic musician during **Bob Marley Week**.

Spice up your Jamaican experience at the Kingston **Curry** Festival in November. **Fishing** enthusiasts will find their niche at the **Blue Marlin** Tournament in Port Antonio typically during October.

Literary lovers should plan to attend the **Calabash** International Literary Festival, a biennial event that takes place in Treasure Beach.

Visitors might find a **marathon** in Jamaica attracting **runners** from around the globe, offering a unique race experience set to the rhythm of reggae music. Some might even be along the scene coast, combined with the uplifting music, making it a truly unforgettable race.

FESTIVALS

```
L S D A N C E H A L L A S A T
T C A L A B A S H Y R R U C
J A Z Z N D D N R L N H I O
A R Z N O E T U B I R T B S
R N L O H R C O E T T E G T
E I I I T D A N C E S C N U
G V N T A A N I U R E N I M
G A G A R T S M M A F E H E
A L B R A U Q N Q R M I S S
E B O B M A R L E Y U R I E
G R S E E L A V I T S E F N
K Y L L R U N N E R S P O U
B L U E M A R L I N V X P T
R S E C N A M R O F R E P P
```

- Blue Marlin
- Bob Marley
- Calabash
- Carnival
- Celebration
- Costumes
- Curry
- Dance
- Dancehall
- Dazzling
- Experience
- Festival
- Fishing
- Jazz
- Literary
- Marathon
- Music
- Performances
- Reggae
- Runners
- Sumfest
- Tribute
- Tunes

27. BEACHES

When it comes to paradise on earth, Jamaica's beaches set the benchmark. **Seven** Mile Beach in Negril is a stretch of pristine white sand and crystal-clear waters perfect for sunbathing and swimming.

Boston Bay Beach is renowned for its exhilarating surf and spicy jerk cuisine. Then there is **Burwood** Beach in Trelawny with a laid-back vibe and picnic-perfect scenery. In Montego Bay, there is **Doctor's Cave** with its pristine waters, rumored to have therapeutic properties. The calm, turquoise waters of **Cornwall** Beach are ideal for snorkeling.

Hellshire Beach is known for its authentic seafood offerings. Other must-visit beaches include **Treasure** Beach and Reggae Beach. **Lime Cay** is a peaceful escape accessible by boat, shouldn't be missed. Experience the rustic beauty of **Pleasure Cove**, a lesser-known spot perfect for a quiet getaway.

But the allure of Jamaica's coastline doesn't end there. From the vibrant energy of **Aqua Sol** and the tranquility of **Bloody Bay** to the iconic splendor of **James Bond** Beach and the hidden gem of **Frenchman's Cove**, Jamaica offers a diverse array of coastal experiences.

For ultimate relaxation, visit **Pellew Island**, also called Monkey Island, an isolated yet breathtaking beach near Port Antonio. **Puerto Seco** Beach in Discovery Bay offers modern amenities, making it perfect for families, while the serene shores of **Runaway Bay** promise warm waters and unforgettable sunsets.

Whether you're exploring the natural beauty of **Bluefields**, the family-friendly shores of **Turtle** Beach, **Fort Clarence** or **Low Cay** Beach, each location promises a unique blend of adventure and relaxation, making Jamaica a dream destination for beach lovers worldwide.

BEACHES

```
E R E V O C E R U S A E L P
V P R Y G O T U R T L E I E
O J I A T H R N E V E S M L
C V H B A Q U A S O L Q E L
S P S N B U R W O O D V C E
N U L O H L S A N S A N A W
A E L T J S T Y R A N I Y I
M R E S D N O B S E M A J S
H T H O T R E A S U R E X L
C O R B Y A B Y D O O L B A
N S B L U E F I E L D S Z N
E E W E V A C S R O T C O D
R C O R N W A L L O W C A Y
F O R T C L A R E N C E Y N
```

Aqua Sol
Bloody Bay
Bluefields
Boston Bay
Burwood
Cornwall
Doctor's Cave

Fort Clarence
Frenchmans Cove
Hellshire
James Bond
Lime Cay
Low Cay
Pellew Island

Pleasure Cove
Puerto Seco
Runaway Bay
Seven
Treasure
Turtle

28. WATER ACTIVITIES

From tranquil beaches to thrilling water sports, Jamaica offers endless experiences.

No trip is complete without visiting its world-famous **beaches**. Start at Doctor's Cave Beach in Montego Bay, where crystal-clear waters invite refreshing swims. For more privacy, head to Seven Mile Beach in Negril to swim and explore **marine** life.

For a nature experience, venture to Dunn's River Falls in Ocho Rios. Climb **cascading falls** with pools that offer cool relief along the way. Consider **bamboo rafting** on the Martha Brae or the Rio Grande rivers for peace and tranquility.

Visit Blue Hole, also in Ocho Rios, to **swim** in turquoise waters, **leap** from cliffs, or simply take in the serene beauty. For a unique **nocturnal** experience, head to the Luminous Lagoon near Falmouth, where the waters naturally glow at night.

Jamaica is a playground for **water sports** enthusiasts. Try **scuba diving** among vibrant **coral reefs** and colorful marine life, or **snorkel** to get close to underwater wonders. Prefer to stay above water? Consider **kayaking** or **paddleboarding** along the coastlines.

For adrenaline junkies, motorized sports like **wakeboarding**, water skiing, **tubing**, and **banana boat** rides offer thrills. **Glass-bottom** boat tours allow you to see the **ocean** floor without getting wet.

If you're interested in **fishing**, there are ample opportunities for bottom fishing or **deep-sea** adventures. Charter a **private** boat for breathtaking ocean views and the chance to reel in marlin, tuna, or mahi-mahi.

WATER ACTIVITIES

```
V G N I D R A O B E K A W P
S L L A F G N I D A C S A C
L T U B I N G K Y A K D O C
M A R I N E R A R A D R W D
O L S N O R K E L L E A P T
T A V S W I M A E A E B B A
T N G A N I R B O F P U O O
O R N G S P O R T S S C S B
B U I X N A P S Q R E S E A
S T H P R I V A T E A L H N
S C S D O M V Z L A R O C A
A O I N P O U I T O C E A N
L N F R E T A W D X P V E A
G N I T F A R O O B M A B B
```

Bamboo Rafting
Banana Boat
Beaches
Cascading Falls
Coral
Deep Sea
Diving
Fishing

Glass Bottom
Kayaking
Leap
Marine
Nocturnal
Ocean
Paddleboarding
Private

Reefs
Scuba
Snorkel
Sports
Swim
Tubing
Wakeboarding
Water

29. KINGSTON

Nestled in **Surrey** County, enter via **Norman Manley** Airport to visit Kingston, the **capital** of Jamaica.

Stop at **Devon** House, a stunning example of Jamaican Georgian architecture for world-famous ice cream amid lush surroundings.

Explore **Saint Andrew** and the serene charm of **Stony Hill**, with picturesque views and a peaceful escape from city life. Don't miss **Cane** River Falls, one of Kingston's hidden natural gems, perfect for a refreshing dip.

Stroll through **Hope Gardens**, Kingston's largest public green space, or visit **Emancipation** Park, enriched with symbolic art in a reflective atmosphere.

Experience the lively vibe of **Half Way Tree** and **Mandela Park**, bustling hubs reflecting Kingston's vibrant spirit. Head to **Tivoli Gardens**, home to dynamic music and dance traditions. The historic **Ward Theatre**, once a place for cultural performances, still stands as part of Jamaica's story.

Discover **New Kingston**, the city's business district, which balances urban flair with cultural richness or immerse yourself in reggae history at the **Bob Marley** Museum. Also enjoy live performances at The **Theatre Place**, a hub for Jamaica's arts scene.

Kingston's **southern coast** offers unforgettable experiences with scenic destinations like **Red Hills** and the cultural tapestry of **Rae Town**, famous for its weekend street dances featuring ska, reggae, and dancehall.

KINGSTON

```
S T S A O C N R E H T U O S
K I A V I A O I M O H V P T
R V I A D P R N A P E B N O
A O N R E I M E N E A O O N
P L T E V T A E C G T B T Y
A I A S O A N R I A R M S H
L G N L N L M T P R E A G I
E A D L W Y A Y A D P R N L
D R R I O S N A T E L L I L
N D E H T S L W I N A E K N
A E W D E A E F O S C Y W B
M N R E A L Y L N Q E A E P
C S U R R E Y A J V C A N E
O R E R T A E H T D R A W O
```

Bob Marley
Cane
Capital
Devon
Emancipation
Half Way Tree
Hope Gardens
Mandela Park
New Kingston
Norman Manley
Rae Town
Red Hills
Saint Andrew
Southern Coast
Stony Hill
Surrey
Theatre Place
Tivoli Gardens
Ward Theatre

30. MONTEGO BAY

Montego Bay, affectionately known as **Mobay**, **Jamaica**, offers a delightful blend of beach vibes, historical richness, and natural beauty that's perfect for tourists, beach lovers, and history enthusiasts alike.

Start your adventure at **Doctor's Cave** Beach, renowned for its crystal-clear waters and soft white sands—a haven for sunbathers and swimmers. For those who arrive via **Sangster** International Airport, the excitement of Mobay is just a quick drive away.

History buffs will appreciate **Burchell** Baptist Church and the historic **Greenwood** and **Rose Hall** Great Houses, all offering a glimpse into Jamaica's storied past. Don't miss a visit to **Sam Sharpe** Square, which stands as a tribute to one of Jamaica's national heroes and a pivotal figure in the fight for freedom.

For a taste of local culture, wander down **Gloucester** Avenue, where vibrant **shops** and **eateries** line the streets. The nearby **St. James** Parish Church, with its architectural elegance, adds a spiritual dimension to Mobay's rich historical tapestry.

The lush **landscapes** of the **Croyden** Plantation and **John's Hall** provide a serene escape into the countryside, while **Bellefield** and **Ironshore** offer picturesque settings that capture the essence of Jamaican charm. Ironshore, in particular, is known for its stunning views and luxurious accommodations, perfect for those seeking a touch of indulgence.

Finally, you can unwind at **Cornwall** Beach. Each of these must-visit spots ensures that your time in Montego Bay is filled with unforgettable experiences. Whether you're drawn by the history, the beaches, or the vibrant culture, Mobay has something for everyone.

MONTEGO BAY

```
K Y R E T S E H C U O L G
X I J O H N S H A L L I S
N S A M S H A R P E J G E
S T M O B A Y G C O A R P
L J A N E D Y O R C M E T
L A I R O N S H O R E E R
E M C O R N W A L L S N E
H E A S P O H S A T I W T
C S O E A T E R I E S O S
R U M H N O A D C Y R O G
U E V A C S R O T C O D N
B E L L E F I E L D H G A
M W L L A N D S C A P E S
```

Bellefield
Burchell
Cornwall
Croyden
Doctors Cave
Eateries
Gloucester
Greenwood
Ironshore
Jamaica
Johns Hall
Landscapes
Mobay
Rose Hall
Sam Sharpe
Sangster
Shops
St. James

31. ROSE HALL

Nestled amidst the lush landscape of Montego Bay, Jamaica, the Rose Hall **Great House** stands as a testament to the island's rich **history** and **colonial grandeur**.

Built in the late 18th century, this **Georgian mansion** and former **plantation** is famed not only for its stunning **architecture** and **breathtaking views** of the **Caribbean** Sea but also for the legend of the "**White Witch**," **Annie Palmer**, who is said to have murdered multiple **husbands** and continues to **haunt** its halls.

With its **grand** staircases and opulent interiors, Rose Hall offers an immersive glimpse into the **past**, capturing the essence of a bygone era where elegance met intrigue.

Visitors to Rose Hall can explore its lavishly decorated **bedrooms**, learn about its storied past through guided tours, and experience the **eerie** allure that has made it one of Jamaica's most popular tourist attractions.

The estate is surrounded by **lush** gardens and provides sweeping vistas that are perfect for those in search of serenity and natural beauty.

For those keen on experiencing the supernatural, the night **tours** offer a heightened sense of mystery and anticipation, as the **shadows** cast by candlelight seem to dance with the spirits of the past.

Whether you're a history buff eager to uncover the stories hidden within its walls, a fan of **ghost** stories seeking a thrill, or simply in search of a **majestic** view, Rose Hall promises an unforgettable experience that combines the allure of history with the excitement of legend.

ROSE HALL

```
R H C T I W E T I H W I N Y
G R A N D E U R G T N E L E
E O R R R N I N S E V T A R
O C E I E X A A G I P N I U
R M E P E M P E E H S U L T
G A S L S A L W B Y Z A R C
I N U A D J S A R B I H D E
A S O N N E H M P N I G E T
N I H T A S A A O E H R R I
D O T A B T D L A O I S A H
N N A T S I O V S E R N O C
A P E I U C W T N U F D N R
R I R O H I S T O R Y E E A
G A G N I K A T H T A E R B
```

- Annie Palmer
- Architecture
- Bedrooms
- Breathtaking
- Caribbean
- Colonial
- Eerie
- Georgian
- Ghost
- Grand
- Grandeur
- Great House
- Haunt
- History
- Husbands
- Lush
- Majestic
- Mansion
- Past
- Plantation
- Shadows
- Tours
- Views
- White Witch

32. NEGRIL

Nestled on Jamaica's **western coast**, Negril is a **vibrant** destination that offers a **perfect** blend of relaxation and **adventure** for cultural explorers and thrill-seekers alike. Known to be a prime **honeymoon** spot, it's a place where **romance** and thrills coexist.

Renowned for its **pristine Seven Mile** Beach, visitors can **bask** in the warmth of the **sun** while enjoying the **crystal clear** turquoise waters. The beach is a hub for **fun**, whether you're dreaming of lounging under the sun or participating in **thrilling** water sports. And with **boats** available for hire, there's an entire ocean to **explore**, turning any day at the beach into an adventure at **sea**.

For those seeking a touch of history, the Negril **Lighthouse** stands as a **beacon** of the island's maritime heritage, providing panoramic **views** that are simply breathtaking. This **landmark** isn't just a sight to behold; it's a window into the past, set against the stunning backdrop of the open **ocean**.

No trip to Negril would be complete without a visit to **Rick's Cafe**, where you can watch fearless **cliff divers leap** into the azure sea as you savor some of the best **sunset** views in the Caribbean.

Whether you're lounging on the **beach**, exploring historical landmarks, or chasing adrenaline-pumping activities, Negril is a place where every corner holds the promise of romance, fun, and new discoveries.

NEGRIL

```
I A M E E N I T S I R P T E
L M P C X I O S W E I V C H
R A A N P E L O N C E I E S
A G E A L S G O M R I B F L
E N L M O N W P N Y K R R E
L I I O R N E E E S E A E S
C L M R E I S F R T O N P U
O L N D M U T A U A N T O O
D I E D N M E C T L O T O H
S R V S N F R S N E C S C T
T H E U U J N K E W A A E H
A T S F F I L C V A E O A G
O S T S R E V I D B B C N I
B N E B A S K R A M D N A L
```

Adventure	Explore	Ricks Café
Bask	Fun	Romance
Beach	Honeymoon	Sea
Beacon	Landmark	Seven Mile
Boats	Leap	Sun
Clear	Lighthouse	Sunset
Cliff	Ocean	Thrilling
Coast	Perfect	Vibrant
Crystal	Pristine	Views
Divers	Renowned	Western

33. OCHO RIOS

Nestled on the **northern coast** of Jamaica, Ocho Rios offers an enchanting blend of **adventure** and **relaxation** that caters to every type of traveler.

For the adventure seekers, the thrill of climbing the iconic **Dunn's River** Falls or ziplining through the lush rainforest canopy is simply unmatched. Embark on a whitewater **rafting** escapade along the **Rio Bueno** River or take an exhilarating **ATV tour** across scenic trails for a dose of adrenaline.

Beach lovers will find their paradise on the golden sands of Turtle Beach, where the azure waters of the Caribbean invite you for a **swim** or **snorkeling** adventure. For a quieter experience, visit **James Bond** Beach, renowned for its crystal-clear waters and Hollywood history.

Family vacationers can delight in a day at **Dolphin Cove**, interacting with friendly **marine** life, or exploring the vibrant flora and fauna at the lush **Shaw Park** Gardens.

Spend an afternoon at **Mystic Mountain**, where you can ride the Jamaican bobsled, a thrilling roller-coaster through the rich rainforest. Kids and adults alike can also enjoy **fun** water activities at **Margaritaville** or stroll through the peaceful **Konoko** Falls and Park, learning about Jamaican culture and history.

History buffs once visited the charming **village** of **Harmony Hall**, an old plantation estate. Another must-see is **Firefly House**, the former home of the famous playwright Noel Coward, offering breathtaking **views** and a glimpse into Jamaica's literary past.

Food enthusiasts should explore the local Jamaican flavors. Visit **Scotchie's**, an iconic spot for jerk chicken and pork.

OCHO RIOS

```
N I A T N U O M C I T S Y M
O O R R E V I R S N N U D A
I O R A F B O K O N O K O R
T M N T F K E Q T L E R L G
A U V E H T T A Z L N A P A
X T I I U E I V C A I P H R
A R L P E B R N B H R W I I
L U L X O W O N G Y A A N T
E O A M I W S I C N M H C A
R T G N I L E K R O N S O V
A O E D N O B S E M A J V I
S E I H C T O C S R D S E L
V E R U T N E V D A T V T L
N U F I R E F L Y H O U S E
```

Adventure
ATV
Beach
Dolphin Cove
Dunns River
Firefly House
Fun
Harmony Hall
James Bond
Konoko
Margaritaville
Marine
Mystic Mountain
Northern Coast
Rafting
Relaxation
Rio Bueno
Scotchies
Shaw Park
Snorkeling
Swim
Tour
Views
Village

34. SHOPPING

Before you leave this beautiful island, make sure to grab some memorable keepsakes that capture the spirit of your visit.

No trip to Jamaica is complete without a bottle of authentic Jamaican **rum**. Be sure to pick up a bottle of Appleton Estate or Wray & Nephew Overproof Rum. **Rum Punch** is also great to recreate cocktails at home.

For **coffee** lovers, Jamaican Blue Mountain Coffee is a must-have. Grown in the misty Blue Mountains, this smooth and mild coffee is considered one of the best in the world.

Jamaica is bursting with talented artisans who produce stunning handmade **crafts**. Look for intricately carved wood pieces, vibrant **paintings**, and beautiful **jewelry**, including **earrings**, **bracelets**, a **necklace**, or **bangles**.

Bring the taste of Jamaica to your kitchen with authentic **jerk** seasoning and spicy hot sauces or even a **cookbook**. Local markets and grocery stores will have a wide selection to choose from.

Support local artists by purchasing their **art** or **music** CDs. Reggae music, synonymous with Jamaica, will help you relive your island memories every time you press play.

Explore local boutiques and markets to find colorful **clothing** and textiles that represent Jamaican style. From bold patterns to lightweight fabrics, these items are perfect for adding a touch of island flair to your wardrobe back home.

Explore **duty-free** shops, local **marketplaces** and **craft markets**, across the island to find these treasures.

Happy Shopping!

SHOPPING

```
A F R S T E L E C A R B D
M N A T S G N I T N I A P
S D J E W E L R Y L A V U
C O O K B O O K R E J Q T
H A T R A E E R F Y T U D
W L D A N E C K L A C E Z
T Y Y M G N I H T O L C P
V N V T L I H N C R A N Y
C O F F E E A R R I N G S
E C B A S T F A R C S H I
R M U R U M P U N C H U O
P S E C A L P T E K R A M
```

Art	**Crafts**	**Marketplaces**
Bangles	**Craft Markets**	**Music**
Bracelets	**Duty Free**	**Necklace**
Clothing	**Earrings**	**Paintings**
Coffee	**Jerk**	**Rum**
Cookbook	**Jewelry**	**Rum Punch**

35. WHAT TO PACK

Planning a trip to Jamaica?

Pack light, breathable clothing to keep cool under the tropical sun.

For beach relaxation, don't forget your **swimsuit** or **swimtrunks**, a good **book**, a wide-brimmed **hat**, and ample **sunscreen** to protect yourself from UV rays. A nice big, packable **tote bag** to carry it all in is a good idea.

Remember to bring a **towel** for lounging on the sand and drying off after a refreshing swim. A pair of comfortable **sandals** or **flip flops** will be perfect for sandy shores. If you prefer **beach shoes**, bring those too. A **scuba** set can enhance your underwater exploration if you're keen on discovering vibrant marine life.

If you're up for hiking, pack sturdy, closed-toe **shoes** that offer good support, along with moisture-wicking **athletic wear** to keep you comfortable on the trails. A lightweight, long-sleeved **shirt** and plenty of **bug spray** can help ward off insects in the lush terrain.

Don't forget essentials like a reusable **water bottle** to stay hydrated, **sunglasses** to shield your eyes, and a waterproof **bag** to keep your belongings safe during beach outings and hikes. A **chapstick** with SPF is handy to protect your lips from the sun.

Bringing a portable phone **charger** can ensure your devices are powered up for capturing those unforgettable moments.

Keep your energy up by packing some **snacks** for the trail or beach **picnic** and bring a pair of **earbuds** for some music or podcasts during downtime. Lastly, consider taking a **journal** or sketchbook to capture your thoughts and experiences.

Happy travels!

WHAT TO PACK

```
J A S E O H S H C A E B M A
I S G S W I M S U I T C S S
R C A A H A R W A I N H F E
A U B G B I P I C N I C O S
E B E L A A R M V R D K R S
W A T E R B O T T L E C F A
C A O E O R S R I E A I L L
I J T O L E A U E W R T I G
T O K E O Y S N S O B S P N
E U N H R O T K A T U P F U
L R S K C A N S A N D A L S
H N N E E R C S N U S H O I
T A Y R A R E G R A H C P N
A L T Y A R P S G U B O S F
```

Athletic Wear
Bag
Beach Shoes
Book
Bug Spray
Chapstick
Charger
Earbuds

Flip Flops
Hat
Journal
Picnic
Sandals
Scuba
Shirt
Shoes

Snacks
Swimsuit
Swimtrunks
Sunglasses
Sunscreen
Tote Bag
Towel
Water bottle

DISCLAIMER

The recommendations provided in this guide by Elloree Press are suggestions only and users must assume their own risk. Elloree Press assumes no liability or responsibility for injury, loss, or damage to persons or property, inconvenience, delay, or expense arising from or caused by any of the third parties referenced herein or by any of the locations included in this book or for weather conditions, acts of God, war, illness, accident, government restrictions or regulations, from an act or omission of any individual, traffic or road conditions, mechanical problems or any other cause or condition beyond the control of Elloree Press. Elloree Press aims to provide you with travel information and we simply act as your referrer and make recommendations based on our experiences and research but you are solely responsible for travel and visits and acting upon our recommendations. All content and information in this book and in any related marketing materials are for information, education and entertainment purposes only and does not constitute formal travel advice or instruction. We strongly urge you to do your own due diligence into the companies and locations referenced to check carefully in full before you book them. There are always certain inherent risks involved in any travel such as physical injury, equipment failures, inaccessibility to medical attention and difficulty in evacuation from remote locations in case of a medical emergency. You agree to assume all travel risks associated with your travel and itinerary. You also agree that we shall not be held liable for any damage, loss, delay, expenses, or inconvenience you may experience that's beyond our control through the acts or omissions of any supplier, agency or operator we use or recommend for all the services and/or products referenced.

Elloree Press has no special knowledge of risks or dangers during travel to or at any destinations referenced herein and disclaims any liability or claims for losses of any kind. For information related to such dangers, we recommend going to the State Department travel website at www.travel.state.gov, click on "Find International travel Information" then click on "Country Information", and fill in the name of the destination country prior to travel.

ANSWERS

1. WHAT TO EXPECT

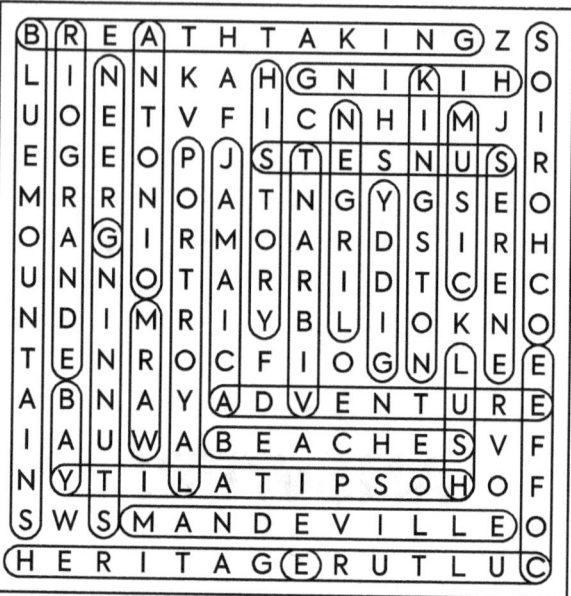

2. HISTORY OF JAMAICA

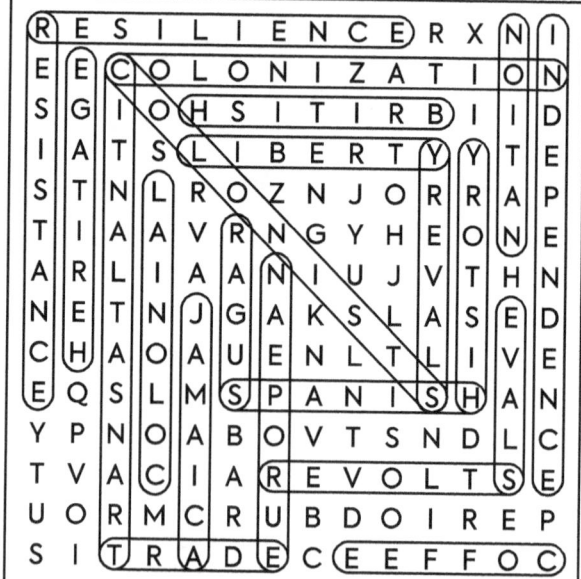

3. JAMAICA IS KNOWN FOR

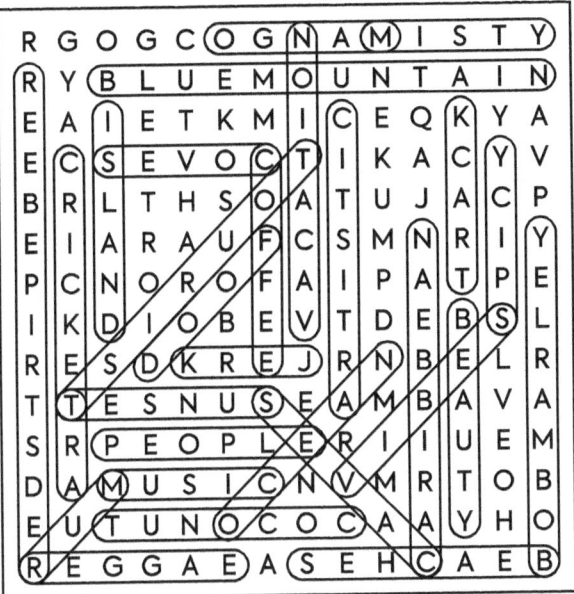

4. JAMAICAN PEOPLE

5. MAGIC OF JAMAICA

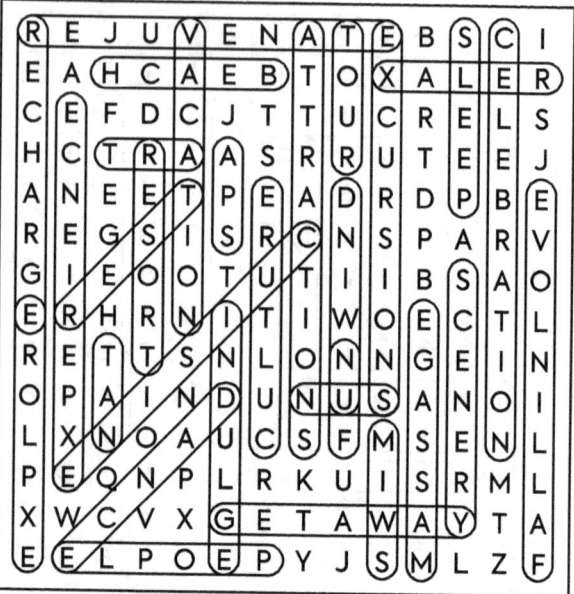

6. LITTLE KNOWN FACTS

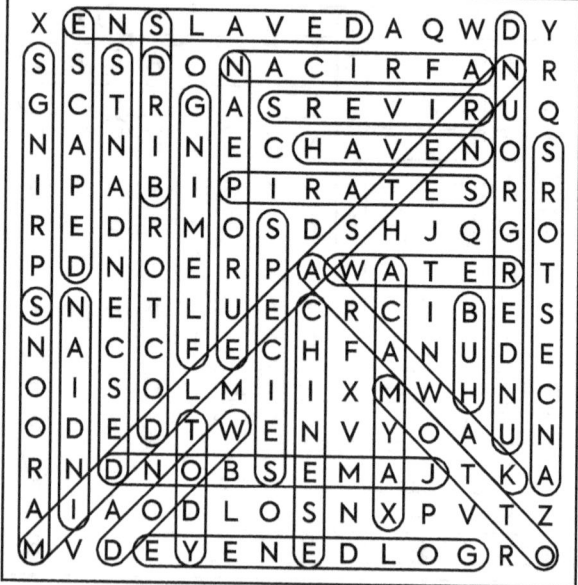

7. JAMAICA ON SCREEN

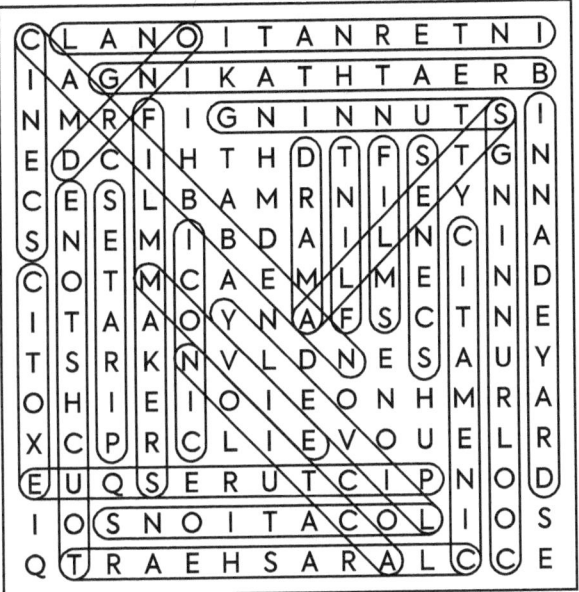

8. ECONOMY & INTERNATIONAL TRADE

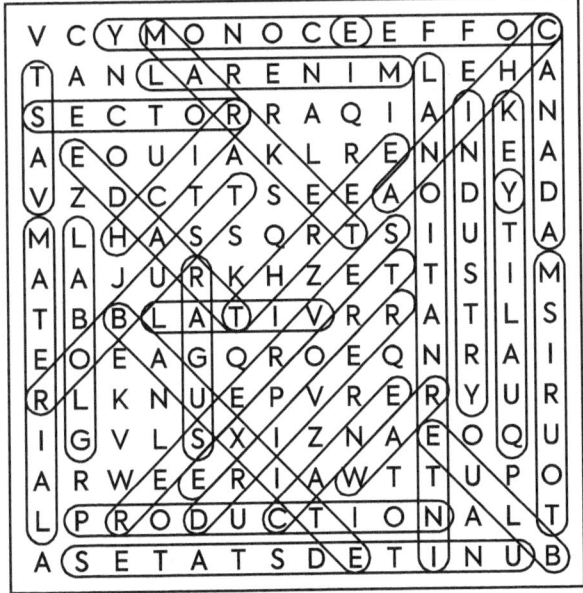

9. POLITICAL FIGURES

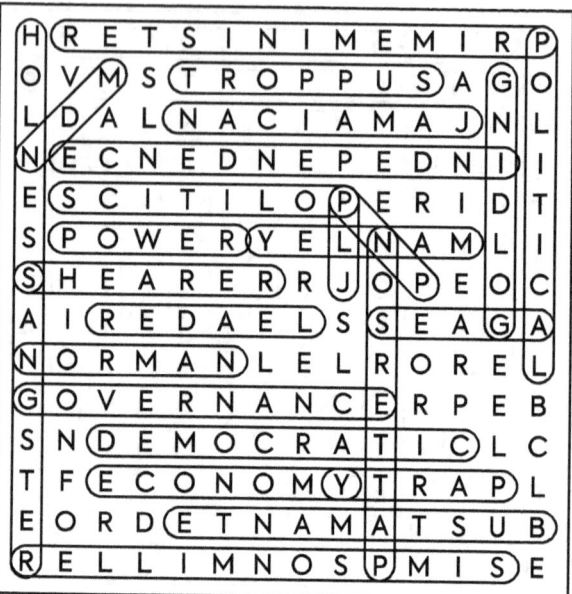

10. SAM SHARPE

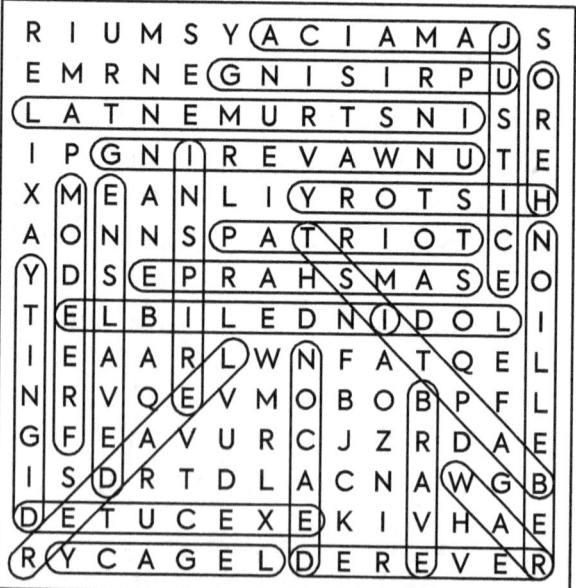

11. MARCUS GARVEY

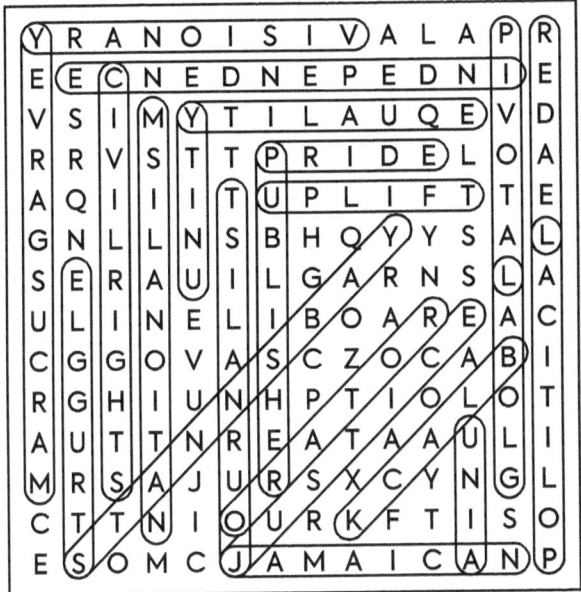

12. BOB MARLEY

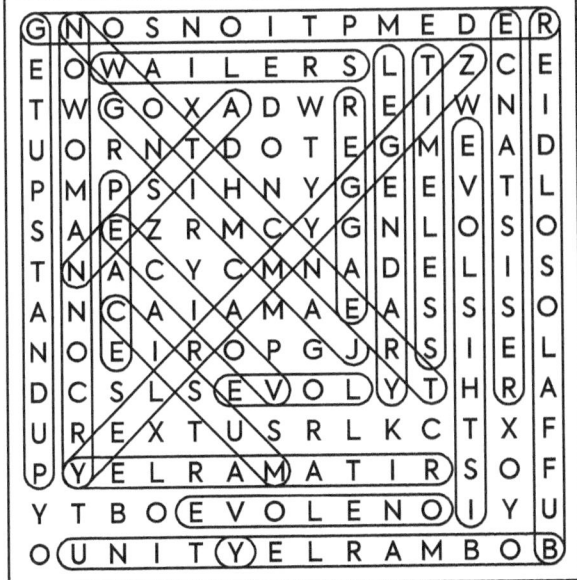

13. MUSIC ARTISTS

14. SPORTS ICONS

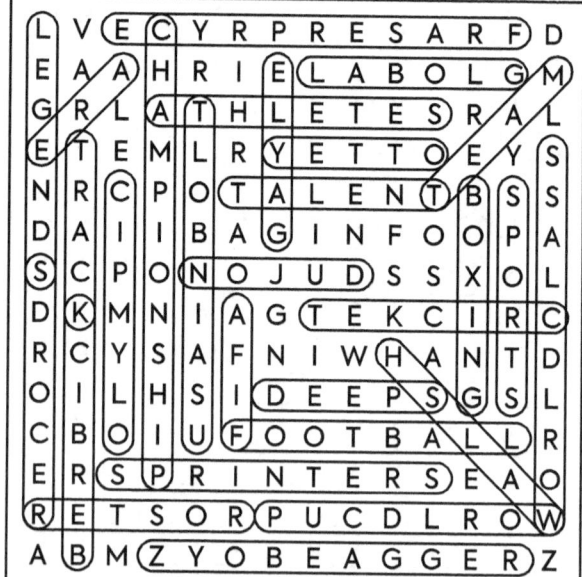

15. USAIN BOLT

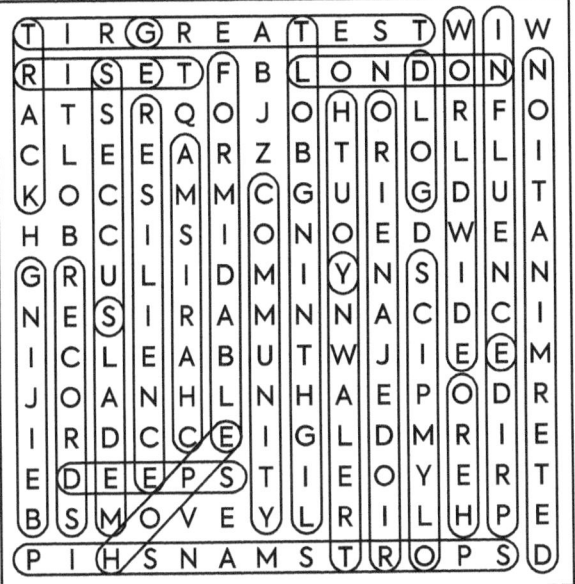

16. ROOTS IN JAMAICA

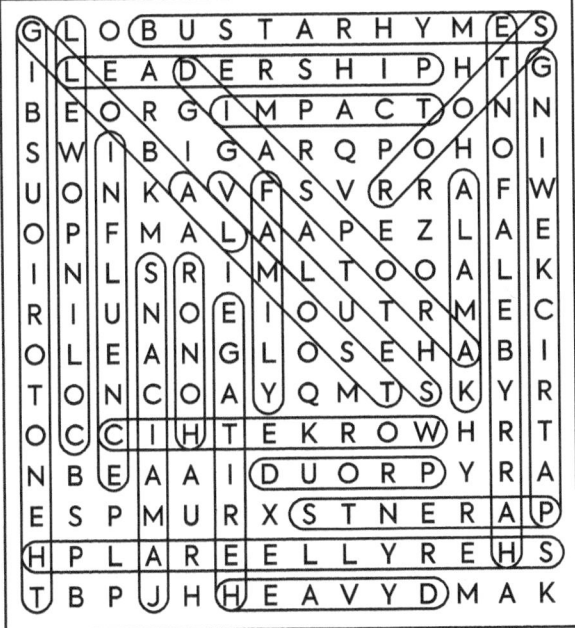

17. FOOD

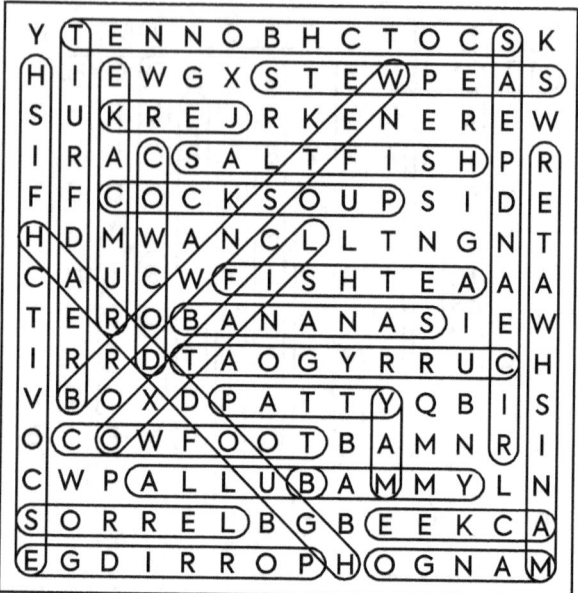

18. REGGAE MUSIC

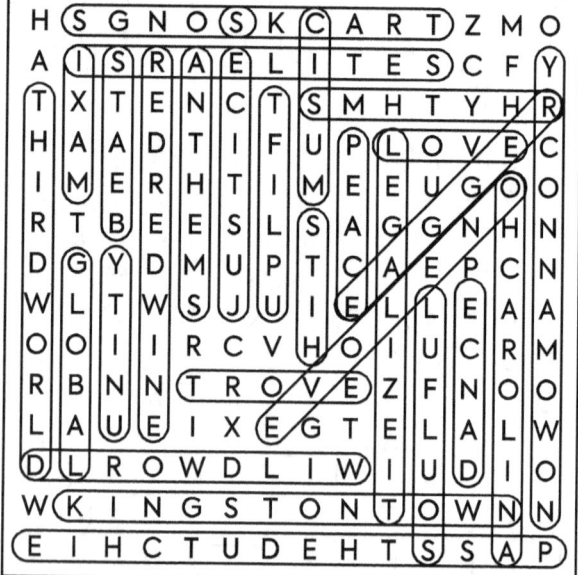

19. RASTAFARI

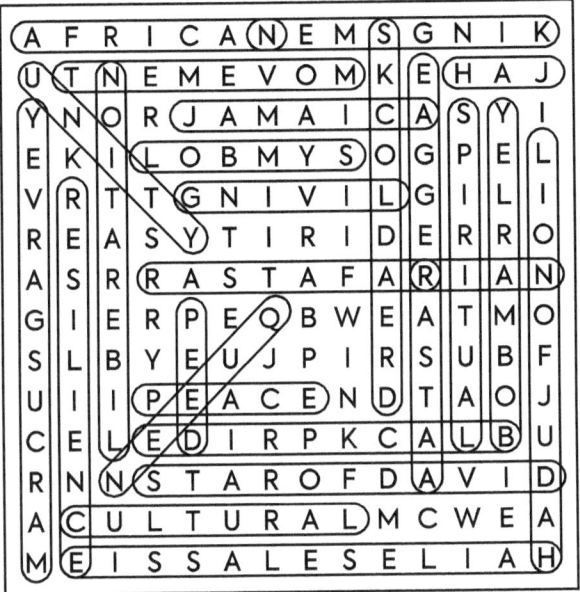

20. JAMAICAN ART

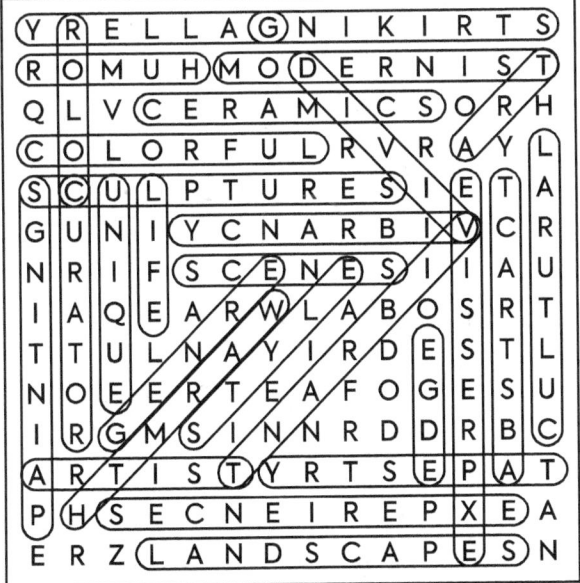

21. FLOWERS

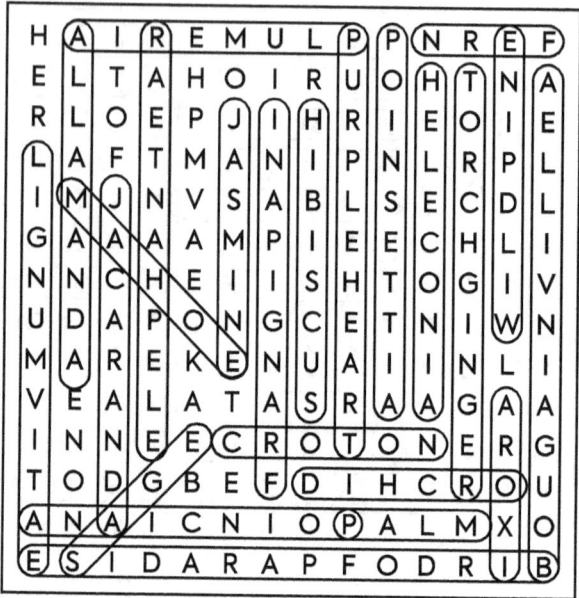

22. ORGANICS

23. PATOIS

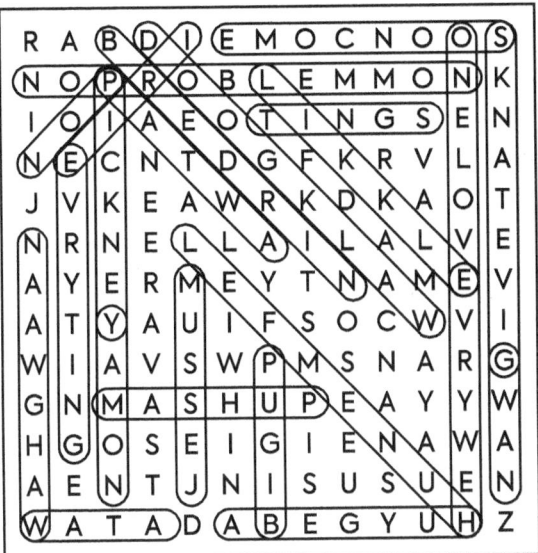

24. THINGS TO DO IN JAMAICA

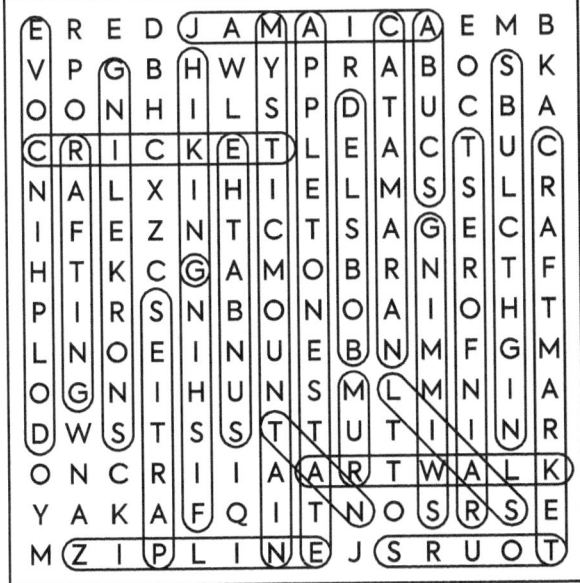

25. MUSEUMS AND CULTURAL SPACES

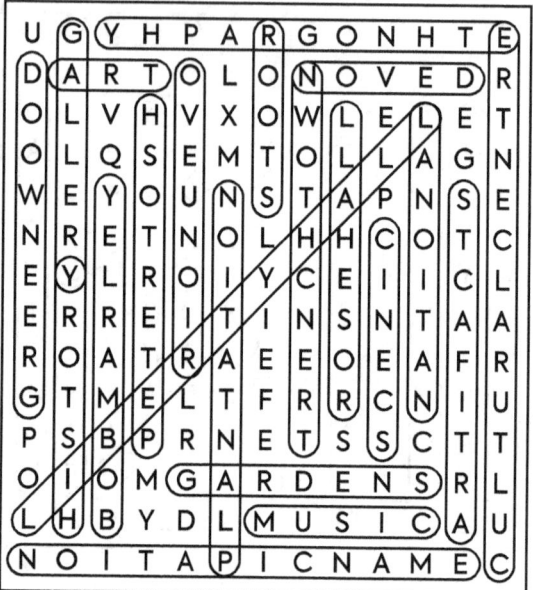

26. FESTIVALS

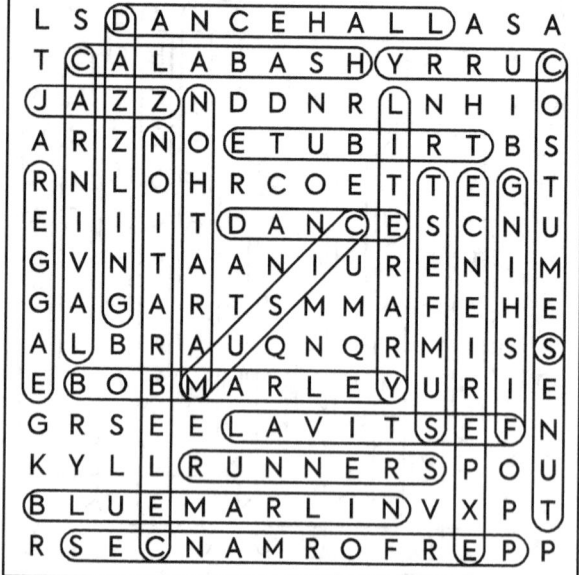

27. BEACHES

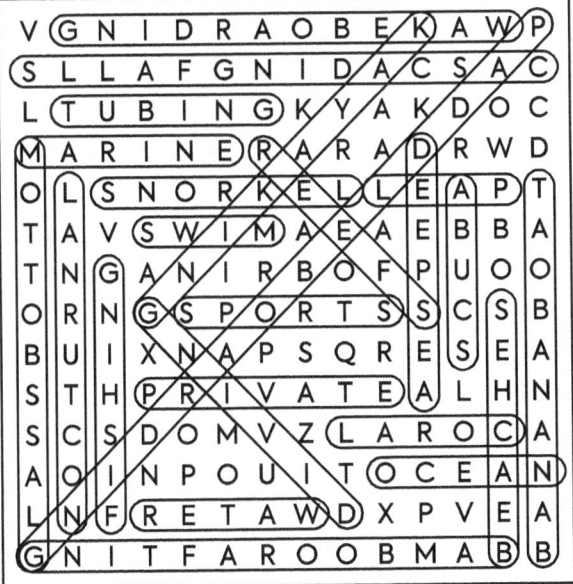

28. WATER ACTIVITIES

29. KINGSTON

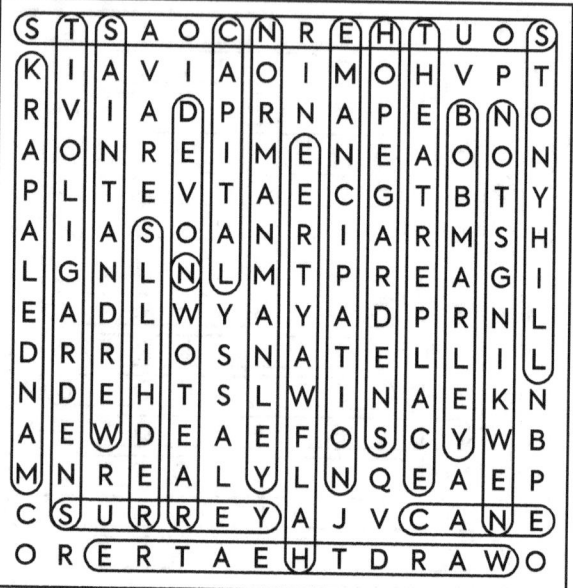

30. MONTEGO BAY

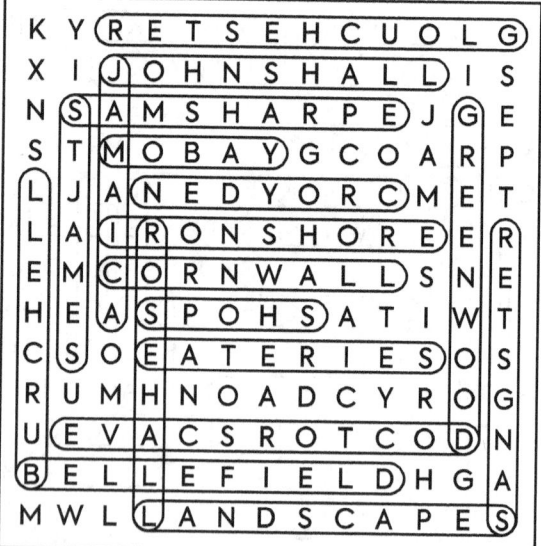

31. ROSE HALL

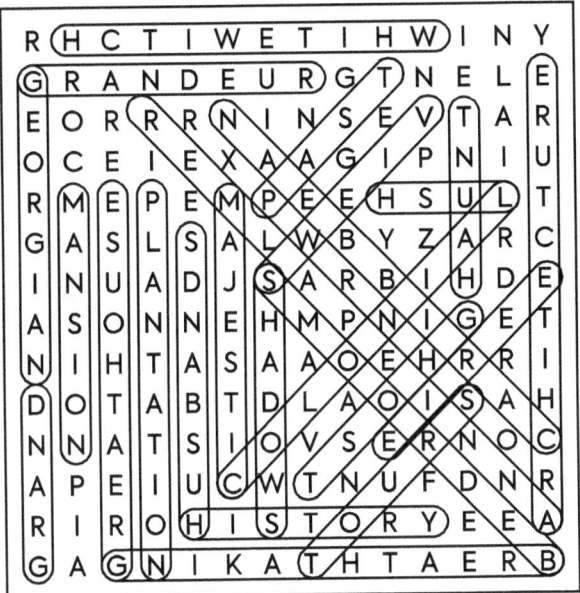

32. NEGRIL

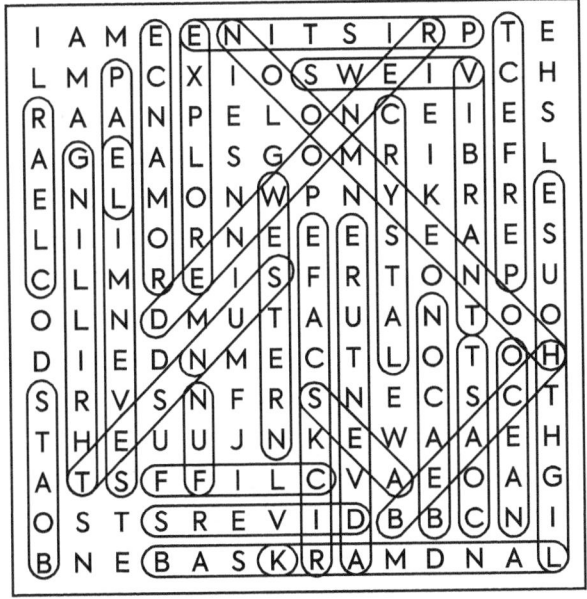

33. OCHO RIOS

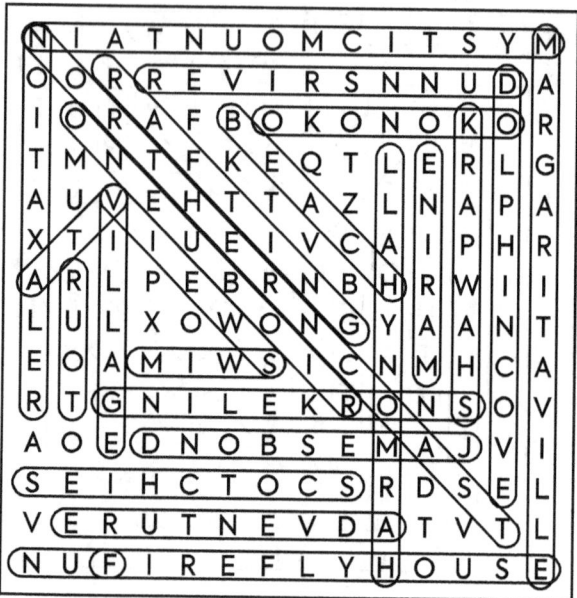

34. SHOPPING

35. WHAT TO PACK

www.ingramcontent.com/pod-product-compliance
Lightning Source LLC
Chambersburg PA
CBHW050441010526
44118CB00013B/1623